Northamptonshire Walks with Children

Judy Smith

Dedication

For Amy and Ben (ages undisclosed!) who so much
enjoyed going for a walk with a checklist!

Contents

The Walks

Quick Reference

Plan your day at a glance with this chart and the location map which follows, to check which routes have the features or facilities you require. For more information, see the individual route.

Notes and Key

Bus: routes that start within a short distance of a bus stop

Cafe: cafe or tea room along the route or very close to it

Pub: pub along the route where families are welcome

Wet Weather: routes with hard surface all the way round, suitable for all weather conditions

Flat: route is more or less flat, little climbing required

Historical: places or features of historical interest along the route

Pushchairs: walks with at least part of the route suitable for pushchairs.

Features: places of specific interest to families along the route

	Bus	Cafe	Pub	Wet Weather	Flat	Historical	Push-chairs	Features
1. Oundle	✓	✓	✓		✓	✓	✓	Dragonfly Museum; Peacocks; Country Park
2. Brigstock	✓		✓			✓	✓	Forest with deer; Saxon Church; Country Park
3. Great Addington			✓			✓		View of 12 churches; Bronze Age tumuli; Water Mill on river
4. Castle Ashby	✓	✓	✓			✓	✓	Stately Home; view along Nene Valley
5. Stoke Bruerne	✓	✓	✓			✓		Canal Centre; locks; museum
6. Pattishall	✓		✓					Fine views
7. Silverstone	✓		✓			✓		Woodland with picnic area
8. Aynho	✓		✓			✓	✓	Apricot trees; paddling in brook; attractive villages
9. Middleton Cheney	✓		✓					Good views; church with fine stained glass
10. Boddington			✓			✓	✓	Reservoir; Midland Thorns
11. Fawsley			✓			✓		Landscaped parkland; bluebell wood; attractive village
12. Flore	✓		✓		✓			Canalside walk
13. Brixworth	✓	✓	✓			✓	✓	Brampton Valley Way; Countryside Park; Saxon church
14. West Haddon	✓		✓					Pretty village; good views
15. Barby	✓		✓					Fine views
16. Welford	✓		✓			✓		Canal Wharf; Deserted Medieval village; Sulby Abbey ruins
17. Arthingworth			✓			✓	✓	Brampton Valley Way; railway tunnels; good views
18. East Carlton		✓	✓			✓	✓	Countryside Park; exhibition; good views
19. Wakerley			✓	✓		✓	✓	Woodland centre with picnic tables; excellent views
20. Yarwell	✓		✓			✓		Old mill and lock on River Nene; Prebendal Manor; stepping stones

Location Map

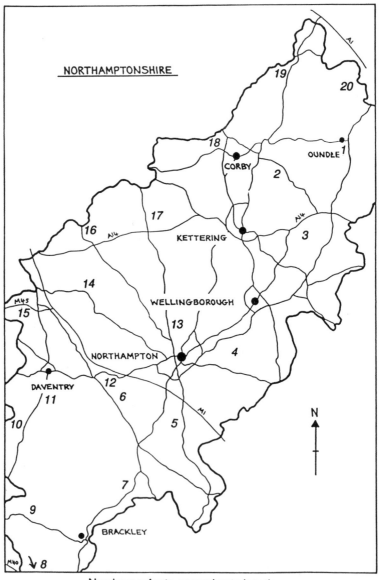

Numbers refer to approximate locations;
see previous page for features and facilities

Walking with children

In this book you will find 20 short circular walks, none of them longer than 6 miles. Each walk starts from an area of recreation, has a sketch map and route description, and gives you an indication of the refreshment stops you might make en route.

But these are walks with a difference! Firstly, you will be given a 'checklist' – a tally of things which you are likely to see on your way. We cannot, of course, guarantee that they will all be waiting for you – rabbits and pheasants have a habit of moving around! But you should have an excellent chance of spotting most of them. Then, there are a few questions to be answered as you go. For each question and each item on the checklist there are points to be gained, and at the end of the day, your overall score merits a comment! You will even find answers to the questions at the back of the book should you need them! But certainly, if you prefer, there is no need to score at all – the walks are all enjoyable for their own sakes.

If I could offer just one piece of advice, it would be that you should take your time. Children do not understand hurry, and it is your aim here to encourage a life-long interest in walking! Make a day of it, take snacks with you, buy sweets or ice-cream where there is a shop, take a picnic or have a meal at the suggested pub. Each walk starts from a Country Park or Playing Field where any extra time may happily be spent at the end. Where parking at a village playing field has been suggested, the relevant permission has always been sought and you are more than welcome.

Typestyle conventions

This book is intended to be read by both parents and children. The following conventions have been used to make the book easy to use:

⇒ Directions (intended for adults) are in this typeface.

☺ Information with the smiley face in the margin is for the children – either to be read aloud, or for them to read themselves.

Q5 Questions look like this; "Q5" is question 5 in a particular walk.

Answers to these questions are in the back of the book. Space is provided after each question to write down the answer. Write down the score for the answers in the spaces provided so that you can add up the total score at the end of the walk.

Enjoying the countryside

Here is some advice to help you and others gain the most enjoyment from the countryside:

℧ Do not drop litter. If you cannot find a bin, take your litter home.

℧ Close all gates after you (unless they were tied open when you found them) so that animals do not stray on to the road.

℧ Keep your own dog on a lead when there are farm animals around.

℧ Stick to public footpaths, and do not wander on to private land.

℧ When walking on a road, always walk on the right-hand side so that you face the oncoming traffic. Keep well in to the side and walk on the verge where possible.

℧ Do not pick wild flowers. They should be allowed to grow and multiply in the countryside.

℧ Do not eat, or put in your mouth, any berries or toadstools you may come across. It is difficult to tell which are poisonous!

℧ Take care near water, and remember that rivers and canals can be quite deep. Stay away from the edge!

A Note about Public Rights of Way

Every parish in Northamptonshire has a Parish Path Warden who looks after all the footpaths. So each route in this book should be clear and you should have no difficulty following the waymarks. Just occasionally you may find crops growing across a path. When these reach a certain height, they must be cut to restore the right of way. You have a right to follow the path at any time of the year, but if you find it difficult, do not hesitate to take an alternative route around the edge of the field. Ploughing time can cause similar problems, when for a short time the path may be obliterated. The excellent waymarking in Northamptonshire should point you in the right direction at this time. Any difficulties you do encounter should be reported to the Rights of Way department of Northamptonshire County Council, Tel. **01604 237582**.

Bus Information and Tourist Information Centres

It is not always easy to find information on bus services in Northamptonshire! The main operator is United Counties, tel. 01604 620077. However, Tourist Information Centres are often helpful with this and many other enquiries. The main ones are listed below.

Northampton: 01604 622677

Brackley: 01280 700111

Corby: 01536 407507

Daventry: 01327 300277

Kettering: 01536 410266

Oundle: 01832 274333

Walk 1: Oundle

A walk beside the river to meet the peacocks

Oundle is a fine old market town – a jumble of mellow stone buildings crowned by the 200 ft (61 metre) spire of St Peter's Church. Its narrow streets are lined with antique shops, old inns and tea-rooms – and, of course, the buildings of Oundle School.

The walk starts from Barnwell Country Park, just south of the town. The park is a most attractive area of grassland and lakes beside a loop of the river. There are tables for picnics and space for playing, while the award-winning Visitor Centre offers a wealth of attractions for children. When you can tear yourself away, the walk starts out along the Nene Way, following the meandering river through its water meadows. The way leaves the river to visit the enchanting estate village of Ashton, where peacocks wander freely, and the *Chequered Skipper* will provide you with a fine feast for a picnic on the green.

A short stroll across fields returns you to Oundle. Your walk will take you along the length of the main thoroughfare and through the Market Square. It is then but a short distance back to the Country Park for some more exploration!

Starting Point: Barnwell Country Park, which can be found on the old A605, half a mile south of Oundle. Grid Ref. 036874

Parking: At Barnwell Country Park.

Distance: 4½ miles.

Map: O.S. Landranger 141, Kettering and Corby; O.S. Landranger 142, Peterborough

Terrain: Grassy riverside paths and short section on cross-field paths. Walk of approximately 1 mile through the town of Oundle.

Public Toilets: At Barnwell Country Park and in Oundle.

Pushchairs: Only the section through Oundle town is suitable for pushchairs.

Refreshments: The *Chequered Skipper* at Ashton is in a picturesque setting beside the village green on which there are oudoor tables for customers. Children are also welcomed inside. Oundle itself is well provided with cafes and inns for refreshment. There are pleasant picnic tables at Barnwell Country Park.

Checklist – score 2 points for each one spotted:

1   A swan
2   A flock of geese
3   A heron
4   A warning sign (a triangle on a yellow background)
5   A rabbit warren
6   A squirrel
7   A pheasant
8   A peacock
9   Someone fishing
10   A narrow boat
11   An 'Old Manor'
12   The date 1877

Total Score _____

Boats on the River Nene

The Walk

⇒ Leaving Barnwell Country Park, turn right (away from Oundle) and follow the footpath alongside the main road for about 200 metres. After the river bridge, cross the road and follow the Nene Way signs down a path beside the river.

☺ Now it's time to keep your eyes open! You will have to be quick off the mark for the first question, and very sharp-eyed, too!

Q1   The Nene Way is a long-distance path, following the river for 67 miles through Northamptonshire. On what date did this section of the Nene Way open? _____

Score 3 points _____

⇒ Your walk now continues on the Nene Way for some 2 miles. Soon you cross over the river at a lock, and shortly afterwards the path briefly leaves the riverbank to cross a field, only to return immediately! The path then sticks beside the river, passing under Oundle by-pass and then describing a wide curve to the left.

☺ The water meadows beside the river make good grazing for cattle – and often flocks of geese are seen grazing too. In summer narrow boats and cruisers ply the river on their way to and from Peterborough and the fens. You may get the chance to be a 'gongoozler' – a name the boaters give to people who stand by to watch a boat passing through a lock!

☺ Just to keep you busy as you go along, you might care to do a little counting!

Q2   After you cross under the by-pass, and before you reach the village of Ashton, how many stiles do you climb over? _____

You can fill in the answer and make a score when you get to Ashton!

☺ And now enjoy that lovely long riverside walk!

⇒ Eventually, the Nene Way crosses the river on a green metal bridge and reaches the road at Ashton Mill.

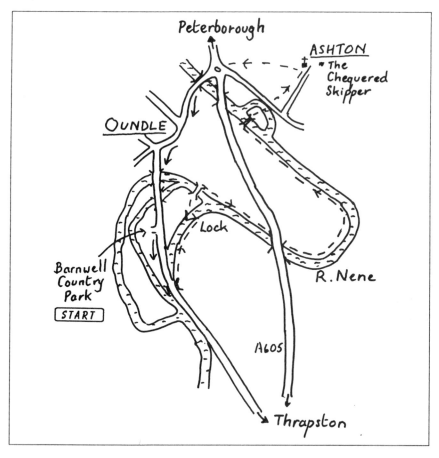

The mill now houses the 'National Dragonfly Museum'. Well, you won't find one of these anywhere else, so if you have the time and it is open, stop and have a look. There is also a tea-room where you can get refreshments.

⇛ Continue by following the Nene Way signs across the road, up a bank, and over a field to Ashton.

Q2 (again!) Have you counted all those stiles? Now is the time to make a score. The answer is in the back as usual, but make sure you write your own score in before you look!

Score 3 points if correct, 1 point if nearly correct! _____

☺ At Ashton you are at least half-way around your walk. It is a very pretty village of thatched cottages – an estate village built around 1900 by Lord Rothschild. He was a generous and up-to-date man and made sure all his workers' homes were equipped with something that was a rare luxury in those days- a bathroom! He also provided them with running water and electricity generated at Ashton Mill. The pub is in the centre of the village and was named by Lord Rothschild 'The Chequered Skipper'.

Q3   *What sort of creature is a 'Chequered Skipper'?* _____

Score 2 points _____

☺ You won't find a live chequered skipper in Ashton – or anywhere else – as unfortunately they are now extinct! But one unusual creature you may see is a peacock! Sometimes there are whole flocks of them wandering around! They belong to the estate.

☺ The village of Ashton has one other claim to fame. Every Autumn it hosts the 'World Conker Championships"! This is great fun to watch!

Q4   *Why do you think Ashton is a good place to hold this event?*
_____

Score 2 points _____

⇛ When you have had a good look around Ashton, return to the church (on the left as you entered the village). Take the footpath through the churchyard and cross over the stile into the field beyond. Walk through this field keeping the woodland on your right.

☺ This small patch of trees seems at times to be alive with creatures. Rabbits are everywhere, as are pheasants, and you may be able to spot a squirrel, too, and make a good score!

⇛ Leave the field by a waymarked stile in the bottom hedge, and follow the footpath with the hedge on your right to a small spinney. The path goes through the trees and then down beside the hedge to come out by the roundabout. Cross the roundabout with care, and take the road to Oundle town centre.

Q5 Soon, you cross the river on a stone bridge. From here, how can you tell the depth of the water? _____

Score 2 points _____

⇒ Keep walking straight ahead along the road.

Q6 On your way through Oundle, try counting the animal head doorknockers you can see. I can't be sure exactly how many there are, but there are several before you reach the Market Square.

_____

Score 1 point for each knocker _____

⇒ Go straight ahead at the War Memorial.

☺ Oundle is a fascinating town, and everyone might like to explore more. There are plenty of cafes where you can take a break!

⇒ Keep to the main road as it bends to the left, and continue alongside it downhill and over the river bridge. In about 200 metres, some steps on the right lead you back into Barnwell Country Park.

⇒ On your way back to the car park, try one last challenge!

Q7 Can you find a post with the white letters 18 Z on it? It is well concealed!

Score 3 points _____

Well done! And now for that score . . .

More Than 35   Excellent! Very sharp-eyed!

20 – 35   Very good indeed!

Under 20   Better luck on your next walk!

Walk 2: Brigstock

A deer hunt through the forest

Brigstock is an ancient settlement of Rockingham Forest, a vast woodland which once covered the north of the county. The forest was the hunting ground of Norman kings, who had a hunting lodge built in Brigstock in 1150. Despite the efforts of these ancient Royals, deer are still plentiful in the forest and you may well see some on your walk. There are both fallow deer and the tiny muntjacs.

The route starts from Brigstock Country Park where there is a Visitor Centre and a playground for children. From here, you climb up a hill with magnificent views before entering Fermyn Woods, now managed by the Forestry Commission. The woodand is a lovely cool place on a hot summer's day and is full of interest. A variety of trees, shrubs, flowers and lichens throng the well-marked paths, and, of course, it is a haven for wildlife – you can see their footprints in every patch of damp earth.

Emerging from the forest, the route passes an airfield occupied by a gliding club and on a fine weekend you can watch these graceful planes circling in the air or witness the excitements of launching and landing.

After the airfield, another section of forest paths brings you back into the old village of Brigstock. Here there are possibilities for refreshment, with two pubs and a village store. The village itself merits exploration. The central square with its Elizabethan market cross and lovely stone houses is most attractive, and you should not miss the church, famous for its Saxon tower which is one of the oldest in Britain. A footbridge over the road returns you directly to the Country Park.

Starting Point: Brigstock Country Park, Grid Ref. 953850. The Park is signed off the A6116 Thrapston – Corby road east of Brigstock.

Parking: At Brigstock Country Park

Distance: 4 miles

Map: O.S. Landranger 141, Kettering and Corby

Terrain: Grassy tracks and woodland paths. The latter can be muddy, especially in winter. Pavements through village.

Public Toilets: At Brigstock Country Park

Pushchairs: Not suitable, except for short section in village.

Refreshments: The *Green Dragon* at Brigstock welcomes children. It has a small outside beer garden. The *Three Cocks* also in Brigstock caters for children in the bar area. There is a well-stocked small supermarket in Brigstock opposite the *Three Cocks*.

Checklist – Score 2 points for each:

1   A pond
2   An oak tree
3   An ash tree
4   An old bath!
5   A house with the name of a tree
6   A glider
7   A wooden bridge
8   Lichen
9   A squirrel
10   A picture of a bomber aeroplane
11   Deer footprints
12   This building

and – for 5 points –

13   A deer!

Total Score_____

The Walk

⇒ From the car park at Brigstock Country Park, take the path which goes uphill along the right-hand side of the play area. The path soon leaves the park at a waymarked stile in the hedge on the right and crosses the field diagonally towards a point of woodland over the top of the hill. From this woodland corner, take the obvious diagonal path to another corner of woodland ahead beside a tall tree.

☺ As you climb, turn around and look at the fine view behind you.

Q1   For each church spire that you can see, score 1 point. _____

Score _____

⇒ At this second woodland point, ignore the footpath ahead and turn left following the woodland edge.

☺ The hedge on the left is full of blossom in the spring, followed by berries later in the year.

Q2   Find 3 different shrubs in the hedge. If blossom or berries are present your task will be easier! Score 1 point for each.

_____ ____

Score _____

⇒ Take the second footpath on the left which turns into the wood.

☺ Hundreds of years ago, English kings would come 'on holiday' to this forest to hunt the deer. Fortunately, the deer have survived to this day — there are now both fallow deer and the tiny muntjacs. Go very quietly if you wish to spot them! You will almost certainly see their cloven-hooved footprints where the ground is wet.

Q3   There is an area to the left of the path which is enclosed by a stout high wire fence. Why do you think such a fence is needed?

_____

Score 2 points _____

⇒ Keep straight ahead on this footpath (there is a little 'kink' in the middle of it) to reach the road. Cross over and continue ahead down the track beside the airfield. At the bottom of the hill, do not cross the bridge, but turn left along the woodland edge. At the corner of the field the path again enters the woodland. Just before emerging at the far side of the wood, take a sharp turn left. Again, just at the woodland edge, take a sharp turn right down a narrow track.

☺ This is a good place for spotting deer!

⇒ This narrow track leaves the forest, and just after emerging you will see a stile on your left. Climb this and cross the field diagonally to the hedge on the right. In this hedge is a well-concealed stile, and over it the waymarked path leads downhill beside the hedge to reach the road. Here, turn left, cross under the bypass, and continue into Brigstock.

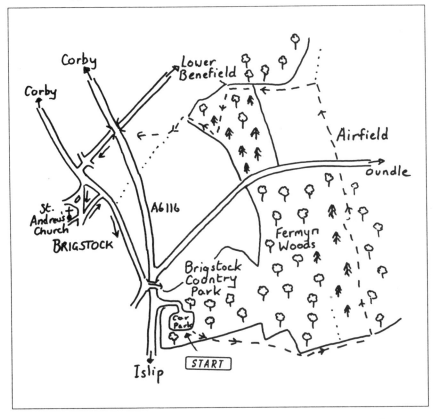

Brigstock village square

☺ As you walk down the hill into Brigstock, look for a wall on the left which has a sign to tell you that here was once the Village Pound – the place where any stray animals were collected and held.

Q4 What animal is shown on the Village Pound sign? _____

Score 2 points _____

⇒ At the junction with the Three Cocks Inn on the right, turn left. 50 metres along the road, turn right into the village square.

☺ The old cross in the centre of the square has carvings on it commemorating the Queens of England. Look for Elizabeth I (E.R. 1586), Queen Anne (A.R. 1705), Queen Victoria (R.H.V.R. 1887 – her golden jubilee) and Elizabeth II (EIIR 1953)

⇒ Continue downhill along Church Street, and take the footpath to the church on the right.

Q5 What feature is seen on the wall, above the porch door of the church? _____

Score 2 points _____

😊 Take the opportunity to look at the curious Saxon church tower with its rounded extension – it is about 1000 years old!

⇒ On leaving the church, go back along the footpath, cross Church Street, and head up The Syke opposite. At the top of The Syke, turn right into Lyveden Road. After 400 metres or so, at a sharp right-hand corner, a path and some steps on the left lead to a footbridge over the road which returns you to Brigstock Country Park.

Well done! And now it's time to look at your score – - -

More than 26   First class!

18 – 26   A good score!

Under 18   Take another walk next week!

Walk 3: Great Addington

Lakes, locks and ancient history in the Nene Valley

The Romans had a villa in Great Addington. The Saxons were there, too, and, before them all, Bronze Age man roamed on the hill above. On this walk you can climb that hill to where Bronze Age tumuli stand on the skyline and look down on a fine view along the lovely Nene valley. The church spires, for which Northamptonshire is justly famous, are at their very best in this valley, and from one viewpoint you can count 10 of them – and two towers as well!

From the viewpoint your route drops down beside the river to the old village of Woodford, where stone houses tumble down the hill, and the church at the bottom is full of interesting stories! You have a choice of two pubs beside the village green to provide you with an excellent lunch, and there is also a village stores.

The return route along the Nene Way is most attractive. Gravel workings in this area have left a series of lakes, now naturalised and home to a wide variety of wildfowl. You will also pass a picturesque old water mill with moorings for river craft and walk beside two locks on the river where in summer you may well see boats working through. This exciting walk in the Nene Valley is packed with interest for everyone!

Starting Point: The Addingtons Playing Field, Grid Ref. 959744. From the A6, turn north at Irthlingborough. The playing field is on the left-hand side of the road between the villages of Little and Great Addington.

Parking: There is ample parking at the playing field.

Distance: 4½ miles

Map: O.S. Landranger 141, Kettering and Corby

Terrain: Cross-field paths and a little road walking.

Public Toilets: None

Pushchairs: Only in village of Woodford.

Refreshments: *The Hare and Hounds* at Great Addington serves excellent meals, but unfortunately only on weekday lunchtimes. Children are very well catered for with a variety of toys and other outdoor play equipment in a private garden. *The Duke's Arms* and *The White Horse* at Woodford both welcome children and each has a small outdoor play area. The village stores is on the main road, 200 metres north of the green.

Checklist – Score 2 points for each

1   A picture of a horse and rider in a triangle
2   A cattle grid
3   A black coach and horses
4   A number 7 in a red circle
5   A cow
6   A war memorial
7   Someone fishing from a boat
8   A millwheel
9   Bronze Age tumuli
10 A clump of beech trees
11 A seagull
12 A bale of hay

Total Score: _____

Upper Ringstead Lock

The Walk

⇒ From the playing field entrance, turn left and walk along the pavement into the village of Great Addington. At the road junction, with the Hare and Hounds on the corner, turn right towards Ringstead. Follow the road out of the village and turn left at a footpath crossing, just after the bottom of the dip.

☺ You are now on the route of the old Roman Road which came from the big Roman camp at Irchester and went to join another 'main' Roman road near Lowick.

⇒ Follow this footpath around the edge of the field and up to a stile in the corner of the next field. Go over the stile and turn uphill immediately over another stile. Continue uphill with the hedge on your right. At the top of the hill, climb over a stile and cross another field diagonally left on the obvious path to come out on the Woodford road.

☺ Where the field path meets the road, climb on to the bank and look around you. You can see lots of church spires! One day there may be a display board to help you find them all, but for now you will have to do it yourself! There are 10 spires in all, but one of them (Rushden) is very distant and cannot always be seen.

Q1   How many spires can you see? (Be honest!) _____

Score 1 point for each: _____

⇒ When you have had enough of spire-spotting, turn right along the road towards Woodford.

☺ Those mounds with trees on you can see across the road are 'tumuli' – Bronze Age burial chambers, over 3000 years old. These have never been properly excavated. People lived in the Nene Valley a long time ago!

⇒ As you walk towards Woodford, you will see a footpath on the left and then a track on the right and, just afterwards, a stile in the hedge on the right. Cross this stile and then the field behind it. Climb over the stile at the bottom left-hand corner of the field into another field and turn left to reach a gate into a lane.

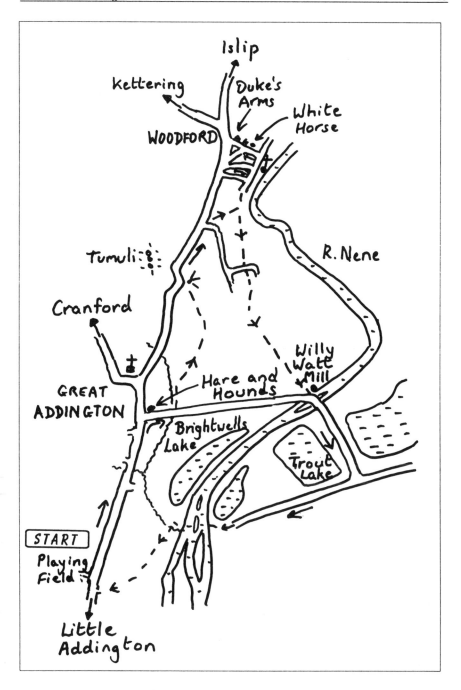

☺ The field on the left just before the gate has an interesting-looking assortment of 'humps and hollows'. These are the remains of a medieval manor which once stood on this site — the notice board will give you the details!

⇒ Go along the lane past St Mary's Church on the right.

☺ Lots of interesting things have happened in this church! Last century, an embalmed heart, thought to be that of a local knight crusader, was found when the church was being restored. You can still see it, now behind glass in one of the pillars. Much more recently, about 35 years ago, the church became famous for its ghost! Two boys, out on a cycle-ride one weekend, took a photograph inside the church. When it was developed, a clear image of a ghost kneeling at the altar was seen. It was never proved a fake, either! Well, you need not worry — he's not been seen since!

⇒ Take the first left after the church (Club Lane) and keep going uphill until you reach the village green.

☺ The old houses around the green make a very attractive scene. The two inns are close by, while the shop, actually a post office, is just up the road to the right. Take time to explore, and, while doing so, answer the next question!

Q2   What number does the blacksmith live at? _____

Score 3 points _____

⇒ Turn left now towards Great Addington and a short way along the road turn left following the Nene Way signs down Pound Lane. You will follow the Nene Way all the way back now.

⇒ At the bottom of the hill, turn right and follow the lane back to the field you came through earlier. Keep straight ahead on the broad track through the field to yet another stile. Go over the stile and carry straight on with the hedge on your right. The Nene Way now crosses a track to the marina and then runs along the bottom of another field. The way then crosses the next field going diagonally uphill and comes out on a long straight track, on which you then continue.

Eventually this long track crosses the route of the disused railway which once ran from Northampton to Peterborough, but closed over 30 years ago.

⇒ After crossing the railway track, cross the corner of a field and come out on the road at Willy Watt Mill. There has been a mill here for centuries – one was mentioned in the Domesday Book – and this one has been used for paper-making as well as grinding the corn. Look for the old wheel on the far side of the building.

☺ On the opposite side of the bridge is a lock. If there is a boat in it you can see how it works – otherwise perhaps an adult with you can explain! The locks on the River Nene are 'guillotine locks' – the guillotine is that big black gate that moves up and down. Canal locks are rather different – you may see some on another walk.

⇒ From the mill, turn left and walk along the road towards Ringstead, with lakes on either side. You can walk on a raised platform on the left. Years ago this part of the river often flooded (it still does from time to time) and it helped to keep people's feet dry!

☺ The lake on the opposite side is a fishing lake stocked with trout. Look out for their 'scarecrow': an orange inflatable man in one of the boats which they switch on when cormorants are around trying to steal the fish. It isn't working all the time, so if you see it you are fortunate – SCORE THE BONUS!

⇒ At the sharp corner, turn right on the road alongside the trout fishery. This is called Station Road – it leads to the old Ringstead and Addington Station, which stood in what is now a clear area at the end of the road.

Q3 Besides trout, what other sort of fish are found in the lake?

_____

Score 3 points _____

☺ The area you are passing through here was again the site of a medieval village – this one called Mill Cotton after the mill which used to stand beside the river.

⇒ Past the station area, keep straight on towards the river. Upper Ringstead Lock is ahead on the left – with another chance to watch a boat passing through! You then cross a bridge over the navigation channel and another bridge over 'Back Brook' – notice the old stepping stones and walkway between them.

⇒ After the second bridge, the Nene Way goes off to the left, while on your right there is Brightwells Lake. Walk to the edge of the lake and have a look. It is usually very popular with wildfowl, and you may see several different sorts

Q4   For one point each, how many different kinds of birds can you see on
      the lake? _____

Score _____

⇒ Now continue on the Nene Way which crosses a ditch and then the field beyond it. A broad track with the hedge on the left now leads uphill to the road.

☺ A Roman villa once stood in the field on the other side of the hedge -if the crops are low you can just see some undulations. No-one has ever excavated here – can you imagine what lies under the soil?

⇒ Turn right on the road to return to the playing field.

_____

Well done! You should have a big score for this walk!

More than 30   Brilliant! What keen eyes!

20 – 30   Very well done!

Less than 20   Go round again!

And if you scored the BONUS . . . Many congratulations!

Walk 4: Castle Ashby

A stately home with a view of the lakes

Castle Ashby House is one of the glories of Northamptonshire – a beautiful Elizabethan mansion set in graceful parkland sweeping down to Grendon Lakes where this walk begins. You can park beside the lakes and perhaps return there for a picnic later. The walk will provide you with many distant views of this fine house as well as the opportunity to see it at closer quarters.

After leaving the lakes, the walk first climbs the hill to lovely Whiston Church from where you have a view for miles along the length of the Nene Valley. When you descend, a bridleway and cross-field path take you to Castle Ashby, a village full of interest. Unfortunately you cannot visit the house, although you can certainly see some of its curious features from outside. But you can visit the splendid gardens and you should stop a while in the 'farmyard' with its craft shops and informal restaurant offering a very different menu. From here you cross parkland and fields (with more views of the house) to the village of Grendon, where a friendly inn and a village shop will cater for all your needs. A short downhill stroll takes you back to the lakes.

Starting Point: Grendon Lakes, Grid Ref. 867602. Grendon lies south of the A45 between Northampton and Wellingborough and is signposted from that road. Just before reaching the village, turn right following signs to Castle Ashby.

Parking: There are several small car parks on the road beside the lakes.

Distance: 5½ miles

Map: O.S. Landranger 152, Northampton and Milton Keynes

Terrain: Quiet roads and cross-field paths.

Public Toilets: In the 'Farmyard' at Castle Ashby

Pushchairs: Possible on road beside the lakes, and on the section through the village of Castle Ashby.

Refreshments: *The Falcon Hotel* at Castle Ashby has a restaurant and also a Cellar Bar where bar snacks are served. Children are welcome. *The Crown Inn* at Grendon serves meals lunchtimes and evenings and caters for children. There is a beer garden for summer; *The Buttery Restaurant* in the Farmyard is well worth a visit!

Extras to take: You might like to take your binoculars for the view across the Nene Valley from Whiston Church!

Checklist – Score 2 points for each

1   A duck
2   Someone fishing
3   A water tower (you will need to be longsighted!)
4   A gargoyle
5   A ford
6   Ridge and Furrow
7   A thatched porch held up by tree trunks
8   A farm 'that must be heaven to live in'
9   A stately home
10   A stone water trough
11   A stone coat of arms over a door
12   A magpie

Total Score _____

Castle Ashby

The Walk

⇒ From any of the lakeside car parks, walk away from Grendon keeping the lake on your left. For part of the way there is a track running between the road and the lake and this makes a pleasant path. There are fine views of Castle Ashby House across the parkland on the other side. After the lakes end, keep straight ahead on the road to the junction.

⇒ Here, turn right and climb the gradual hill. Where the road bends left, keep straight ahead across the field on a waymarked footpath. Pass through the far hedge and keep left around the edge of the next field to reach a gap with stile in the hedge behind the church. Walk through the churchyard.

☺ St Mary's Church is said to be the work of one man, Anthony Catesby. At least, he certainly paid for it and brought the stonemasons from London to come and build it. The work took all of 25 years! The interesting thing is that it has not been altered since − most churches were 're-stored' by the Victorians!

Q1 I did not tell you the age of this church as you can find out for yourself! In what year was the building completed? _____

Score 3 points _____

☺ Before you leave the church, you must go and have a look at that view! Directly opposite you across the valley is Earls Barton, and you can see the church there with its pale tower quite clearly. That tower is famous and people come from far and wide to visit it. It is over 1000 years old and has beautiful Saxon stone ribbing − if you are lucky enough to have binoculars with you, you may be able to pick out the patterns. Farther to the west, you can see Ecton (Ecton Hall was also built by the Catesbys), and beyond that, the outskirts of Northampton. Your map will help you identify many other features.

⇒ Leave the churchyard by the front gate and walk downhill on the path into the village. On reaching the road, turn left, and bear left at the village green to walk uphill on the road. At a left-hand corner, a bridleway continues ahead. Follow it downhill to where a stream crosses at a ford. Shortly afterwards, a waymarked path leads off on the left, crossing the stream on a wooden bridge. Follow the path uphill beside the wood and then across open fields.

☺ There are lovely views from here back towards Whiston.

⇒ At the road, cross straight over and continue, keeping the hedge on your left. The path passes briefly through woodland before descending to farm buildings.

⇒ At the farm, turn right and keep to the track. Soon this bends downhill to the left and then becomes a tarmacked road. Keeping to this, you will pass through the tiny but interesting hamlet of Chadstone. At the main road, turn left on the pavement and in 1km you will reach Castle Ashby.

☺ The grounds of the house are on your right as you walk along. You can clearly see the ridges and furrows of medieval strip farming in the parkland. The plough, turning the soil inwards, created the ridges. The land here cannot have been cultivated since it was 'enclosed' nearly 300 years ago.

⇒ On entering Castle Ashby, keep straight ahead on the road.

Q2   What is the name of the Northamptonshire Girl Guides Headquarters house? _____

Score 3 points _____

Q3   What sort of cows are in the Castle Ashby herd? _____

Score 2 points _____

☺ Soon you will come to the 'Farmyard' with its craft shops and restaurant on the right. But just before it, on the right, a road leads up to the House and Gardens. It is well worth going to have a closer look at the House – you will need to do, to answer the next questions.

⇒ Turn right up the road to the House and Gardens.

Q4   As you walk up the road, you can see a tall tower of the house immediately ahead of you. The tree in front may obscure it a little in summer, but it will come into view as you walk to the right in the direction of the gardens. Around the top of the tower are some letters and a date. What is the date on the tower? _____

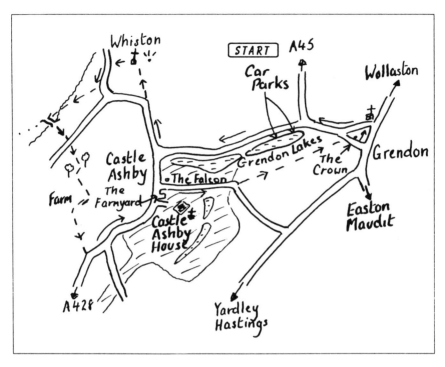

Score 3 points _____

☺ If you walk a little farther on towards the gardens, you will come to the front of the house. It dates from the time of Elizabeth I, and the Compton family who built it were such loyal subjects that they had it designed in the shape of an E in her honour. You will straight away notice all the lettering around the parapets – and even on the garden terraces! There are texts from the Bible in both Latin and English.

Q5 Can you spot CONSIDER THE LILIES ....? Where can you see these words? _____

Score 3 points _____

☺ The earliest lettering was added to the building in 1624, but they got quite carried away with the idea and continued to add it until Victorian times – as you saw on the tower.

⇒ When you are ready – and you may wish to visit the gardens first – walk back down to the road you left earlier.

😊 The 'Farmyard' on you right is well worth exploring!

⇒ Continue along the road as far as the war memorial. Here turn right into the village. At the green with its horse chestnut trees, bear left, and continue ahead on the track which runs downhill through the parkland above the lakes.

⇒ At the bottom of the hill, where the road bends right, continue on the footpath (this may not be waymarked, but there is a stile in the fence) taking you across the field straight ahead. You should be able to see a path across the field, but if not, aim just to the right of Grendon church on the hill. On the far side of the field, a white diamond on a post shows you where a bridge will take you across a ditch into the next field. Cross this field, and then in the third field, head for a passage on the right which you enter by a gate just before the red brick house.

😊 Grendon has some interesting old houses and it is worth taking just a short tour of the village.

Q6   One of the old houses you pass is Blacksmith's Cottage – keep you eyes open for it! How many horseshoes are above its front door?

_____

Score 2 points _____

⇒ Turn right at the main road and head uphill past the Crown Inn. Turn left into Parsons Close.

😊 If you need to find the village shop, you should continue ahead to the end of the road and turn left.

⇒ At the end of the close, continue down a narrow winding passage to come out at another road with the church opposite. Turn left and continue, bearing right at the road junction. Follow this road for about 500 metres (be very careful – there is a short distance without a footpath) At the road junction, turn left, and the lakes are now on your left again.

Well done! Now add up your score – - -

More than 30   First class performance!

18 – 30   Some good work!

Under 18   Come back another day!

Walk 5: Stoke Bruerne

Canal and Countryside

A warm summer's afternoon at Stoke Bruerne, and all is bustle and activity, noise and colour! The brightly painted narrow boats arrive and depart with much shouting and throwing of ropes, the trip boat collects its last passengers before leaving, the hotel boat guests sit on their deck sipping tea. Everyone is having fun – not least the spectators who come to watch the efforts and errors of the boat crews working down seven locks or stand at the dripping mouth of Blisworth tunnel searching the gloom for the lights of approaching boats. Stoke Bruerne is the heart of the English canal system, the mecca which all narrow boat enthusiasts must visit. They come to see the canal museum, which is the very best of its kind, and they come to eat at *The Boat Inn* with a similarly outstanding reputation.

Here it is that your walk starts, and whether it is summer or winter, there is likely to be much to see at Stoke Bruerne. The museum is open almost every day of the year (closed Mondays in winter only), as indeed is the canal shop beside it. You must visit the museum, and you must take time to watch the antics of the boatmen, too, but you must also take a walk. The route described here is just one of many possible from Stoke Bruerne. It is a short walk across the rolling countryside, along field paths and beside woods. Your way passes through the charming village of Shutlanger where the pub can provide you with home-cooked meals and will welcome children. From here, an easy cross-field route brings you back to the activities and excitements of Stoke Bruerne.

Starting Point: Stoke Bruerne wharf, Grid Ref. 743499. Stoke Bruerne lies just west of the A508, 6 miles south of Northampton.

Parking: Roadside parking is prohibited in Stoke Bruerne. There is a car park at the wharf, for which a charge is made. Pub parking is also a possibility for patrons.

Distance: 3½ miles

Map: O. S. Landranger 152, Northampton and Milton Keynes

Terrain: Cross-field paths. Tarmacked roads through village of Shutlanger

Public Toilets: At Stoke Bruerne wharf.

Pushchairs: Not suitable

Refreshments: *The Boat* at Stoke Bruerne is an old establishment, full of character. It caters for children, and also provides a grocer's shop for the necessary ice-cream! *The Navigation,* beside the bridge at Stoke Bruerne, is a modernised pub (now a Mansfield Inn) which is a children's paradise! Children's meals are served and there are most exciting outside and inside play areas. *The Plough* at Shutlanger welcomes children and has a small outdoor play area.

Checklist – Score 2 points for each

1   A cottage with the name of a flower
2   A horse with rider
3   A boat with a bike on top
4   A cat
5   A rugby post
6   A sheep
7   A wood pigeon
8   A plough – or other agricultural machinery
9   A horseshoe
10   A pheasant
11   A round window
12   A wind sock
and – for 4 points –
13   A hare!

Total Score _____

The Walk

⇒ From the wharf, turn right along the canal side (away from the lock) and follow the towpath for about 400 metres.

Q1   How many miles is it to Braunston from here? _____

Score 2 points _____

⇒ Just before the tunnel mouth, take the broad track which leads uphill on the right.

☺ There is no towpath through the tunnel, so, in the days of horse-drawn boats, the horse would have to be led over the top while the boatmen 'legged' the boat through. They would lie on their backs and 'walk' on the ceiling! It took more than 2 hours to get through the tunnel in this fashion – it must have been exhausting work! The track you now walk on was once the path which the horses used. Even before this time, it was the track of a horse-drawn railway. The tunnel was the last part of the canal to be completed, so while it was under construction, goods were taken on this railway between one end of the canal and the other.

⇒ Continue on the track, past the remains of the old railway bridge, to reach the road. Turn right here, and in about 100 metres, take the bridleway signed on the left.

The Canal Museum at Stoke Bruerne

Q2   Looking to your right on the bridleway you can see an old brick
chimney. What do you think is its purpose? (hint – remember that
the canal is underneath!) _____

Score 3 points _____

⇒ Keep straight ahead with the hedge on your right. Eventually the
well-waymarked route bears to the right between two hedges. Again you
keep the hedge on your right and follow it all the way around the field to the
edge of the wood.

☺ This field is very popular with hares! Keep a lookout for them!

Turn left at the corner of the field and walk along beside the wood on the broad
track. At the end of the wood, you will see a gate on your right, but you should go
straight ahead through a waymarked gap into the next field. Continue, keeping
the belt of trees on your right, until you reach the road. Here, turn left and walk
down into Shutlanger.

☺ This must be a very icy place in winter – there seem to be lots of bins
holding salt to thaw the roads!

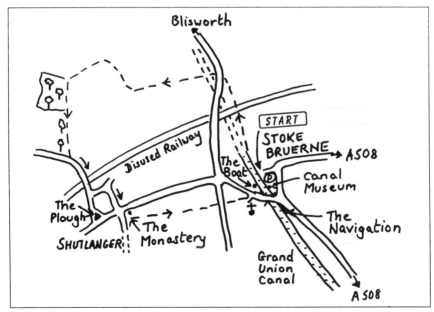

Q3   As you walk through Shutlanger, how many salt bins can you see?

_____

Score 1 point for each. Score _____

⇒ At the first junction, go left into High Street, and in about 200 metres, turn right into Baker's Lane. Follow this lane down over the stream and then uphill to come out at the main road. Cross straight over the main road with care (or turn right along the road if you wish to visit the Plough Inn) and enter Water Lane opposite.

☺ The building on the corner is called *The Monastery* – but quite possibly it never was one! It certainly looks as if it might have been, though! As you walk along the field path in a few minutes, look to the left and you can see the old 13th century porch – it's quite impressive!

⇒ Down Water Lane, take the first footpath signed on the left.

☺ This path crosses a field which was once part of the 'monastery' gardens. From here there are good views over Stoke Park Wood and beyond. On the left, five cut logs have conveniently been placed for you to sit and enjoy the scene!

⇒ The route is now well-waymarked alongside hedges, over a stream and again beside fields to meet the road. Cross the road to a footpath starting 10 metres or so to the right. There may be no waymarker here, but the path is alongside the hedge (keep it on your left) and is usually well-trodden. At the top of the field, you will come out beside some houses with the playing field on your left. Keep straight on across the top of the close towards the church.

Q4   What is forbidden in the churchyard? _____

Score 2 points _____

⇒ The waymarked path does not enter the churchyard, but swings into the field on the left and comes out below the church in Church Lane. Here turn left and then right at the main road. Soon you will arrive at the bridge and the wharf.

Well done! Now count up your score . . .

More than 28   Super-Vision!

20 – 28   Pretty good score!

Under 20   Never mind! Try again!

Walk 6: Pattishall

A three-village ramble

Watling Street, the old Roman road which is now the A5, runs right through the village of Pattishall. But the road reveals merely the tip of the iceberg here – much, much more of Pattishall lies out of sight of the road to the east. This is by far the prettier part, and it is here that you will find a most attractive and fascinating walk.

Pattishall is essentially five villages – Fosters Booth, Dalscote, Pattishall, Eastcote and Astcote – and this walk will take you through the latter three. They are old villages, pleasantly set in rolling countryside, and separated from each other by a wooded valley with a little stream. Above them the land rises, and before Eastcote you will reach a high point where there are views for miles over Northampton to the north and the hilly country of the Heights to the west.

The walk starts from the Village Hall car park, which is beside a large playing field and children's playground. You can picnic here, but there are also opportunities for refreshment at the inn in Eastcote and the village stores in Pattishall. This is a walk full of interest – if possible, take it on a clear day to really appreciate the view!

Starting Point: Pattishall Village Hall, Grid Ref. 677536. From the A5, at Fosters Booth (Pattishall), turn east at cross-roads, signposted to Rothersthorpe. In half a kilometre, turn right, signposted to Astcote. The Village Hall is half a kilometre on right.

Parking: There is lots of parking space at the Village Hall beside the playing field.

Distance: 4 miles

Map: O.S. Landranger 152, Northampton and Milton Keynes.

Terrain: Cross-field paths and village streets.

Public Toilets: None

Pushchairs: Only possible on latter part of the walk through the villages.

Refreshments: *The Eastcote Arms* welcomes children inside and also has an outdoor eating area. *The Red Lion* on the A5 at Pattishall is similarly hospitable and has a beer garden. The Post Office and Village Stores in Pattishall sells a variety of food and is open on weekdays and Saturday mornings.

Checklist – for 2 points each

1   A magpie
2   A house with shutters on the windows
3   A horseshoe
4   A greenhouse
5   A cottage with the name of a flower
6   A cottage with the name of a fruit
7   A radio mast
8   A horse and rider on a weather vane
9   A Coat of Arms (belonging to John de Patteshulle)
10   Northampton Lighthouse (if you don't know what it is, see the text!)
11   A cartwheel
12   A blocked-in doorway (filled in with stone)
     and this time there is an extra *5 points* for the very sharp-eyed who can spot somewhere on the route:
13   A pair of antlers (try looking behind you – or walking backwards!!)

Total Score _____

The Walk

⇒ At the car park entrance, turn right towards Astcote and follow the road into the village.

Q1   On this walk you are going to pass through three villages, so there will be lots of houses and gardens to look at. For every bird table you see on this walk, score 1 point. _____

Score _____

☺ Astcote was once involved in the shoe-making industry – the brick cottage with extension beside the green was a shoe factory. Raw material was collected daily from Northampton and brought to the village where the shoes were hand-made.

Pattishall post office and village green

⇒ Pass the green on your right and the old shop on your left. Coming out of the village, just after Hodge Close, take the bridleway signed on the left. This is called Beggar's Lane and you follow it to its end at a field gate, just after a sharp right-hand bend. Go through the gate and continue along the field with the hedge on your right. At the field corner, turn left and continue on the broad grassy bridleway, again with the hedge on your right.

⇒ The bridleway becomes a lane with high hedges (if it should be autumn, see how many different berries you can find here!) and then follows beside fields to reach Folly Farm.

☺ This undulating area is known as the Flitton Hills

⇒ At Folly Farm, go through the gate and turn left on the lane. With the farm on your left, go round the corner and continue ahead, ignoring the road to Tiffield on the right. Now take the footpath signed on the left, which goes between the farm buildings and past a duck enclosure. On emerging at the field, go straight ahead to a waymarked gap in the hedge opposite. With the white farm on your right, cut across the corner of the next field to a

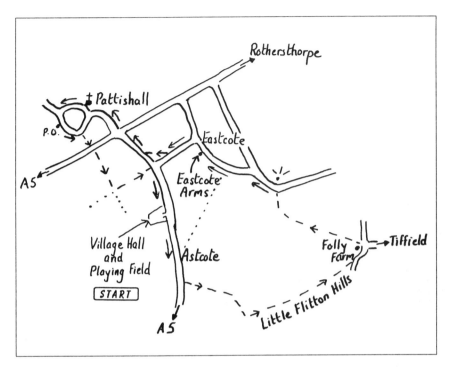

waymarked stile. In the next big field, head uphill to the left of the barn and leave through a tall rusty gate. Continue ahead to reach the road.

🙂 From this road you have magnificent views. Ahead of you to the north is Northampton, where the Express Lifts tower clearly emerges from the sprawling houses. It was Terry Wogan who first called this the 'light-house' – and the name stuck! On the hill behind and just to the left of it, you can see the tower at St Crispin's Hospital, some 5 miles away 'as the crow flies'. If you have binoculars, you can see a lot more. Take time to look around!

⇒ Turn left on the road, and, at the junction, turn left into Eastcote, and walk through the village.

🙂 The broad verges you see on the side of the road here were once used by the villagers for grazing their animals. After the land had been 'en-closed' 200 years ago, this was the only common land left for them.

☺ Don't forget to look out for those bird tables!

Q2 Coming into the village, as the road swings to the right, you will see a cream-coloured house in front of you. It has a very strange name – 'The Old Boot'! Why do you think it might have this odd name?

_____

Score 3 points _____

Q3 Look for a road on the left (before the pub) called 'The Close'. On the left in this road is a house named 'Barton Mead' and if you look a little closer, you will see that it has stone steps beside its front door, and above them, a ring in the wall. What do you think these were used for? _____

Score 3 points _____

⇒ Turn left at the cross-roads after the Eastcote Arms. Keep to the roadside pavement downhill and over the stream at the bottom. Climbing away from the stream, take the footpath signed across the field on your right.

☺ During the First World War, there was a German Prisoner of War camp in this field. The prisoners were all from the navy, and in their spare time, they built a model harbour complete with model boats beside the brook at the bottom of the field. Can you imagine it?

⇒ On reaching the road at the top of the field, turn right. At the crossroads, go straight over into Pattishall, and walk on uphill. Continue ahead, keeping the church on your right, to take a short tour around the village.

☺ There are many interesting old houses and the church itself has features dating from Saxon times.

Q4 What can you see on the wall above the porch door of the church?_____

Score 3 points _____

⇒ At the village green, turn left and pass the Post Office and Stores on you right.

Q5   A little farther on, there is a bench on your left – you might even perhaps stop and eat an ice-cream here if the shop is open. What does the bench commemorate? _____

Score 2 points _____

⇒ Where the road bends left, go up an alley on the right, and then shortly turn left beside a slatted wooden fence. This footpath brings you down to the road again, and you should cross straight over and take the footpath ahead on the other side. Before you reach the top of the hill, another footpath crosses and here you turn left. Cross the field to come out beside the school.

Q6   On the front of the school are some tiles bearing the words 'Pattishall School'. What do the tiles depict? _____

Score 2 points _____

⇒ Turn right on the road to return to the Village Hall.

☺ Have you remembered to count those bird tables? Fill in your score for Q1 now – it could make all the difference!

Well done! It's time to add up your score . . .

More than 30   Absolutely brilliant!

20 – 30   Keen eyes!

Under 20   I didn't think it was that hard!

Walk 7: Silverstone

A foray into the forest

Long before the racing circuit arrived in Silverstone, the village had quite another claim to fame. Silverstone was the main settlement of Whittlewood Forest, and it was here in the 12th century that King John had his royal hunting lodge. In the middle ages the residents were all employed in forest crafts and industries and even today there is a huge timberyard at the heart of Silverstone. There are still remnants of the great forest here, too, and it is in one of these, Bucknell Wood, that your walk starts.

Bucknell Wood is now owned by the Forestry Commission. There is a well-concealed car park beside an attractive glade set out with picnic tables. From here, forest walks are waymarked, but children will love to explore the numerous unmarked paths leading into the deep woodland. One of these leads to a clearing with a picnic table and totem pole – so take along your war paint!

The route takes you right through the heart of the wood where there is always plenty to see. In Spring, look out for catkins and, later on, bluebells. In Autumn, there are berries and fungi. You emerge from the wood on to a farm lane, after which a short cross-field path delivers you to the middle of Silverstone village. Here there is a pub which caters for children, and two village shops which between them can supply just about anything you can think of! Your return to the wood is on a well-marked path across fields of grazing sheep, passing close to the site of a deserted medieval village. Arriving at the main gate of the wood, a narrow track takes you past that totem pole before returning to the picnic area from which your walk began.

Starting Point: Bucknell Wood, Silverstone, Grid Ref 658448. From Silverstone village, follow signs to Abthorpe. The wood is about 1km out of the village on the left-hand side.

Parking: The car park is well-hidden! As you come up to the wood, take the byway leading to the left (if you reach the main gate, you have gone too far!) A barrier prevents you continuing up the byway, but the track here swings right and leads you into the forest car parks.

Distance: 4 miles

Map: O.S. Landranger 152, Northampton and Milton Keynes

Terrain: Forest tracks (can be muddy in winter), cross-field paths and hard-surfaced roads.

Public Toilets: None

Pushchairs: Possible only up the first part of the forest track, and in the village.

Refreshments: *The White Horse* in the centre of Silverstone is a friendly pub, pleased to serve children, and with good-value basket meals. Picnic fare, ice-creams and other treats can be obtained in the well-stocked shops of Silverstone. There is an excellent picnic area at your starting point in Bucknell Wood.

Checklist – for 2 points each

1   A squirrel
2   A pine cone
3   Trees with plastic guards (to prevent animals nibbling)
4   A chicken
5   A horse
6   A weather vane
7   A totem pole
8   A molehill
9   A cart-wheel (look on a gate)
10   A flagpole
11   Football goal posts
12   A wooden five-barred gate

Total Score _____

'Medieval archer' in the forest

The Walk

⇒ From the car parking area, several short paths run through the woodland at the back to join the byway behind. Take one of these and turn right on the byway.

Q1   As you walk along this byway, look at the various trees beside the path. How many different sorts of conifers can you see? _____

Score 1 point for each. Score ____

⇒ Continue on this byway going slightly uphill to reach a big track junction. Here turn left on to the bridleway, which unfortunately can be muddy in winter. Follow this bridleway downhill to where you can see a gate at the edge of the wood (about 50 metres away). At this point a track crosses the bridleway and you should turn left and follow this track to the edge of the wood. Now turn right and very soon you will come to a stile leading into a field. Cross this field and then another stile to come out on a long concrete farm road, on which you turn left.

Q2   The concrete road is long and straight and a series of telegraph poles runs beside it all the way. How many telegraph poles do you pass in total before arriving at the end of the track in West End? Number of poles ____

       (Think hard before you start counting them all – there may be an easier way! But if you find it – beware the change in the middle!)

Score 4 points for correct number (and well done!), 2 points for almost correct.

Score ____

⇒ When you arrive at the road at the end of the track, turn right along West End. Some 200 metres up the road, take the first footpath signed on the left, between the new houses. Follow this footpath over the fields to reach Silverstone village. After the last kissing gate, follow the short lane past the school to emerge on the High Street. Turn left, passing the Post Office, the pub, the newsagent and the church.

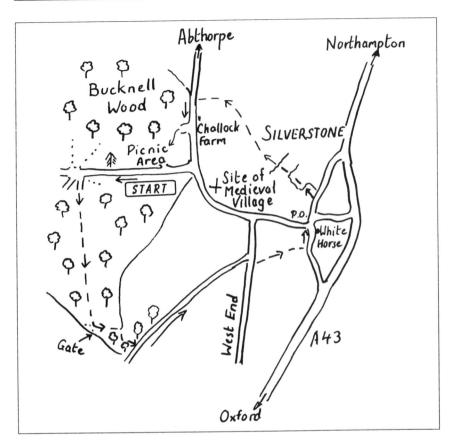

Q3   The big cream house opposite the *White Horse* is quite old. In what year was it built? _____

Score 2 points _____

⇒ Past the church, keep straight ahead into Little London.

☺ In the 1600s, Londoners came to settle in this part of Silverstone to es-
cape the plague in the city—hence the curious name of this road! Some
may well have survived, but the plague was here, too. In a field a little
farther on you will be able to see the humps and hollows which are all
that remain of the medieval village of Charlock, whose inhabitants all
died of the plague. In a way, the same disease was also responsible for
the racing circuit! It is built on the site of a former airfield, which, in turn,

was built on the site of the derelict Luffield Abbey — the Black Death claimed all the monks, too. If you are a motor racing enthusiast, you will have heard of Abbey Corner and Priory Corner — reminders of what lies underneath!

⇒ Take the first footpath on the left (where the road bends gently right). Follow it alongside the stream, and then bear right in the field to cross a wooden bridge. In the next field, follow the direction of the fingerpost. In the far right-hand corner of this field, another bridge will take you across a stream. Now continue straight ahead, up the hill.

☺ From the top, you can see the 'bumpy' site of the deserted village of Charlock over to the left, below the farm (the farm, by the way, is called Challock Farm)

⇒ At the top of the hill, you can see that the hedge ahead of you is met by another hedge coming in from the left. About 50 metres along the hedge to the right of their junction, a stile can just be seen (although it is well concealed!) This stile will lead you to yet another bridge over a stream. In the next field, head straight across to the stile which you can see in the opposite hedge. After this stile, turn left along the hedge to reach the road. Turn left on the road, and shortly turn right at the main entrance to Bucknell Wood.

Q4   Who manages Bucknell Wood today? _____

Score 2 points _____

⇒ About 20 metres inside the wood, take the first small track on the left. This will take you through the wood and past the clearing with totem pole to reach the picnic area again.

━━━━━━━━━━━━━━

Well done! Now have a look at your score . . .

More than 28   Outstanding!

16 – 28   A good effort!

Under 16   Go round again!

Walk 8: Aynho

Woodland, stream
. . . and apricots

Standing in the square at Aynho, with its mellow honey-coloured stone houses, you might think you were in the Cotswolds. And indeed you are – but Northamptonshire's extension of these hills is little known, and is mercifully spared the crowds of visitors!

Aynho is the most southerly village in Northamptonshire. The Cartwright family were squires of the village here for more than 300 years, their home being Aynho Park. The original manor was burned down by royalist troops after their defeat at the battle of Naseby, but Charles I later paid compensation for this, with which money the present house was built. The last squire and his son were killed in a car accident some 50 years ago and the house is now privately owned. Aynho has been called the 'Apricot Village' after the many apricot trees you will see trained against the walls of the cottages. Apparently the squire once accepted them in part payment for rent!

This is a beautiful short walk in rolling countryside. Aynho, and its equally attractive Oxfordshire twin, Souldern, are fascinating. Between them you will pass over meadows and through woodland and cross the pretty Ockley Brook, here the boundary with Oxfordshire. You can also paddle in the brook near Souldern Mill, and this is perhaps a spot for a picnic, although both villages have welcoming pubs. There are other delights on this walk – the pretty village pond at Souldern, the splendid view of Aynho Park as you return, and the cottages of Aynho, their walls clothed with apricot trees.

Starting Point: Aynho village, Grid Ref. 517333. Aynho lies on the B4031, 5 miles south-east of Brackley.

Parking: Roadside parking only. It should be possible to park along Portway, which runs beside the playing field on the eastern edge of the village.

Distance: 3½ miles

Map: O.S. Landranger 151, Stratford-upon-Avon

Terrain: Cross-field paths, hard-surfaced tracks and roads through villages.

Public Toilets: None

Pushchairs: Suitable in villages, and on return track from Souldern.

Refreshments: *The Cartwright Arms* in Aynho and *The Fox* at Souldern are both pubs which welcome children. Only *The Fox* has an outdoor eating area and garden.

Checklist – for 2 points each:

1   A bale of hay
2   A fallen tree
3   A horseshoe
4   A stream that disappears underground
5   A weeping willow tree
6   An old water pump
7   A weather vane
8   A white gate
9   An arched window
10   Village stocks
11   An apricot tree
12   An Old Posting House
and – for a bonus of 5 points:
13   A fish or a tadpole!

Total Score _____

The Walk

⇒ At the end of Portway, cross over the main road (with care!), and take the footpath opposite. The track runs between high walls and finally passes through a short tunnel.

Q1   Occasionally, there are flights of steps leading over or through the wall on the right. How many flights of steps do you pass? _____

Score 1 point for each.

Score _____

⇒ Continue beside a fence on the right to a wood. Past this, two white discs lead you across a field, after which a gate on the left brings you on to a concrete track. Follow the track down and through the woodland to cross a stream. You are now in foreign territory – Oxfordshire! Continue ahead beside a fence, and then aim for a stile to the left of a row of tall conifer trees.

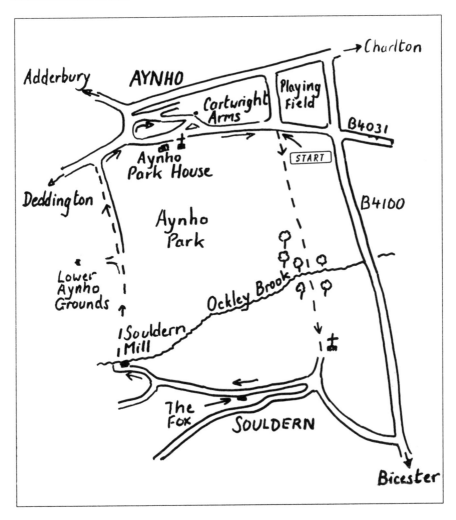

A track beside the stream now brings you out on a concrete track leading past the church.

Q2 What can you see on top of the church tower? _____

Score 2 points _____

⇒ Continue ahead to meet the road.

☺ The very picturesque village pond is on your left – give a thought to scoring some bonus points from the checklist!

⇛ Turn right on the road and walk through the village.

Q3   In Souldern, can you find a house with a clock on the wall, and a house with two baby pelicans (I think that's what they are!) on the roof? _____

Score 3 points for each

Score _____

Souldern church

⇛ Ignore the footpath opposite the Manor House and continue along the road. Where the road swings left, go straight ahead on the concrete track, and continue on this to cross the brook at Souldern Mill.

☺ It could be possible to dip your toes in this lovely clear brook – perhaps while the adults have a seat on the bank beside the footpath!

⇒ When you are ready, continue uphill on the concrete track. Soon you will join the narrow road running to Lower Aynho Grounds Farm, which is on your left. Keep straight ahead with the wall of Aynho Park on your right. Keep to this road for about half a mile to reach the main road.

☺ You will now be following the high wall of Aynho Park all the way back to Aynho. To keep you awake, here are two questions -

Q4   As you walk beside the wall, you will pass some gateways where you can see into the park.

For 1 point each, how many gateways do you pass before reaching Aynho?

_____

Score _____

Q5   At one point you will pass a very strange tree – or is it two trees? The two 'trunks' separate and join again to give what appear to be long slits through the tree trunk. If you can spot this tree . . .

Score 4 points _____

⇒ At the road, turn right and climb the hill into Aynho. At the road junction at the top, turn left past the stocks and cross the road carefully. Turn right into Blacksmith's Hill, and where it forks, keep right.

☺ At the top of the hill is The Square with its lovely old houses. Can you see one with a yew tree growing out of the garden wall?

⇒ From The Square, continue ahead to The Green and the *Cartwright Arms.*

☺ The houses here have apricot trees trained up their walls. The lower branches have all been removed so that the fruit is out of reach for children! Isn't that mean! But the people who used to live here once upon a time had to give the apricots to the lord of the manor as part of their rent, so the apricots were very precious!

☺ Everything around here seems to be 'Cartwright' (did you see the stocks were put up on the orders of a Cartwright, too?) – in fact this corner of Northamptonshire was once called 'Cartwrights' Corner'!

Q6 The Cartwright coat of arms has an animal's head at the top. What
    terrible fate has befallen this beast? _____

Score 4 points _____

⇒ Turn left and follow the main road (passing the Jacobean old grammar
school) to reach the end of the Portway.

Well done! You could have made a big score here . . .

More than 38   Quite outstanding!

24 – 38   Very good work!

Under 24   Go and do it again!

Just for the record, the maximum score here was 53! Did anyone
make it?

Walk 9: Middleton Cheney

A wander in the Wolds

The southernmost tip of Northamptonshire is known to the geographer as 'The Wolds'. The region is, in fact, an easterly extension of the Cotswolds – but without the multitude of visitors! Although the stone is a little darker, the villages here are just as pretty and the same gently undulating country-side can be enjoyed, as you can see on this short walk.

Middleton Cheney is a large village, and one that has grown greatly in re-cent times. The heart of the old village around the church has some fine stone buildings and is a delight to explore. From here you meander over low hills with good views and then drop to the lovely village of Chacombe, nestling in its wooded valley. Here, an old inn, *The George and Dragon*, will serve you refreshment in an olde worlde setting, while the village stores will provide for simpler needs. Leaving Chacombe, you climb yet another hill and return to Middleton Cheney across the fields, guided by the mag-nificent spire of its 14th century church.

Starting Point: Middleton Cheney Playing Field, Grid Ref. 499416. The village lies just north of the A422 Brackley – Banbury road, 3 miles from Banbury. The playing field is in Astrop Road, which you reach by turning south, away from the village at the war memorial cross-roads.

Parking: There is a small car park beside the playing field.

Distance: 3½ miles

Map: O.S. Landranger 151, Stratford-upon-Avon

Terrain: Field paths and short section on quiet road.

Public Toilets: None

Pushchairs: Not suitable

Refreshments: Middleton Cheney is a large village with shops of all kinds and two pubs near the centre of the village. `The Dolphin and The Red Lion both serve meals at lunchtimes only, and both have a special children's menu. The George and Dragon at Chacombe is a lovely old pub which welcomes children in-side and has an outside eating area also.

Extras to take: There are good views, so a pair of binoculars might come in handy.

Checklist – Score 2 points for each

1 A squirrel
2 A horse
3 The date 1911
4 A golf course
5 An old water pump
6 A round window
7 A dry stone wall
8 A house with the name of a month
9 A cottage with the name of an animal
10 A bird bath
11 The M40
12 This building:

Total score _____

Middleton Cheney church

The Walk

⇒ Leave the playing field and turn right along Astrop Road towards the village of Middleton Cheney. At the cross-roads, cross straight over and head up High Street. After the Baptist Chapel on the left, take a footpath bearing left and, almost immediately, turn right into Church Lane. Now take a grassy lane on the left, just after the stone building and before the shop (Don't worry — you are coming back this way to have a look at the church!) At the top left-hand corner, a well-concealed narrow path leads you beside the wall and over a stile.

☺ On the stile is a picture of a shell, which is the logo of the Jurassic Way — you may have seen it on other walks in this book. The shell is actually a fossil of a creature with the magnificent name of *Kallirhynchia sharpi*, which can be found in rocks from the Jurassic era.

Q1   This question will probably drive you crazy, but we won't be too strict about the answer! You are now about to follow the Jurassic Way from here to Chacombe. How many of these shell signs do you pass? (Count only the ones for travellers in your direction!) _____

If you are nearly correct (you can decide how near!), score 4 points

Score _____

⇒ Over the stile, head downhill over the brook and maintain the same direction uphill afterwards. Keep the hedge first on your right and then on your left to reach the top of the field. Cross straight over the road and then cross the next field in the same direction. Now cross a tarmac track and continue across the next field.

Q2   How many spires can you see as you cross this field? _____

Score 1 point for each spire.

Score _____

⇒ At the top hedge, turn sharp right along the hedge line, following the direction of the signs (Are you still counting them?). Go through an iron gate and on to a rough track.

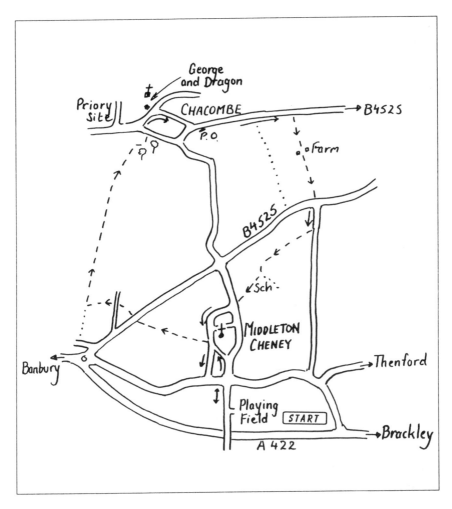

Q3 On the right now are some very curiously shaped trees, all twisted and spreading sideways. They are actually quite common ones, which must have been trained to grow like this. What sort of trees are they? _____

Score 3 points _____

⇒ Continue on the track through more gates, and eventually cross a field heading towards a line of conifers at the top of a hill. The path now passes through an iron kissing gate and into a wood. Emerging from the trees, there are fine views to the west as you continue, keeping the wood on your right.

☺ As you come round the hill, the fine house you see below you was built on the site of an Augustinian Priory which Henry VIII demolished in his purge of 1536. The present house was built not long afterwards, although there have been alterations since then.

⇒ At a stile, turn away from the wood, downhill across a field to another stile in its bottom right-hand corner, beside some sheep-shelters. Cross the small compound, go over another stile and you are again in woodland.

Q4 You are on a path winding beneath some trees which are evergreens. What sort of trees are they? _____

Score 3 points _____

⇒ Follow around the house and reach the road – and pass the last of those shell signs! If you have been counting them, fill in your total now!

Q5 The house on your right is called 'The Old Farmhouse'. As you go through the village, look out for another house whose name starts with 'The Old . . .'. Name of house _____

Score 2 points _____

⇒ At the road, turn left, and immediately right into Thorpe Road. At the junction with the village stores opposite, turn left. Keep on this road out of the village, and then take the second footpath signed on the right (soon after passing Chinner Farm on the left). The grassy track climbs the hill to reach a farm at the top.

⇒ Continue ahead on the farm drive to reach the main road. Cross to the lane opposite and take the first footpath on the right (approximately 200 metres) This clear footpath leads up beside the hedge, and cuts across the corner of the second field to reach the school at the top of the hill. Go through the wooden gate to the right of the school to enter a narrow lane, which runs between the school grounds and the back gardens of houses on the right. Keep straight ahead on this lane, soon with back gardens on the left, to reach the main road. Cross straight over into Glovers Lane and follow it where it bends left to reach the church wall. Continuing ahead will bring you to the front of the church and Church Lane again.

☺ This lovely old church has many interesting features. Unfortunately, it is usually locked, but if you get the key, you can see one of the finest collections of 19th century stained glass windows by William Morris and others. They really are quite remarkable, and well worth seeing. Middleton Cheney was the site of an early battle of the Civil War. It took place not far from the playing field where you may have parked your car. The Parliamentary forces were defeated at this battle (although, of course, they later won the war) and 46 of their men were afterwards buried in this churchyard.

⇒ Continue ahead down Queens Lane to reach the main road. Cross it and go right down Astrop Road to return to the playing field.

Well done! Are you ready for that score . . . ?

More than 28   Eyes like a hawk!

18 – 28   Pretty smart!

Under 18   Not too sharp today!

Walk 10: Boddington

A reservoir walk

In the far east of the county, in the rolling countryside of the Northamptonshire Heights, are the old twin villages of Upper and Lower Boddington. In the last century a small reservoir was created nearby to act as a feeder for the Oxford Canal and it is here that the walk starts.

The route around the reservoir is attractive with plenty to see – especially on a summer weekend when the cheerful boats of the Banbury Sailing Club take to the water. Over the hill is the tiny village of Lower Boddington where the names of the houses tell the story of times long past. Climbing from here to Upper Boddington, there are magnificent views to the west over the Warwickshire plain. If it is a particularly fine day, you might feel inspired after your walk to drive up to the highest point in this area, the hill where the Telecommunications tower is installed. It is said that, on the very clearest of days, the Malvern Hills, some 50 miles away, can be seen

Upper Boddington itself is a lovely old village with a beautiful 15th century church. In each of the Boddingtons you will find a child-friendly pub. In Upper Boddington there is a village stores where you can buy not only a treat for the children, but also one for your dog – it is a pet food store!

The return begins along a very minor road known as Welsh Road. This route was once used by the drovers of Wales taking their cattle to the markets of London. Returning across fields to the reservoir, you come out briefly on a road bordered by ancient hedgerows, where the rare Midland Hawthorn can be found. A short walk along the high north dam of the reservoir then brings you back to the car park.

Starting Point: Boddington Reservoir, Grid Ref. 497534. From the A361, turn west at Byfield (7 miles south of Daventry), signposted to Upper Boddington.

Parking: Reservoir car park on Byfield to Upper Boddington road, east side of reservoir.

Distance: 3 miles

Map: Landranger 151, Stratford-upon-Avon.

Terrain: Well-worn track around reservoir, cross-field paths and quiet roads.

Public Toilets: None

Pushchairs: Possible beside the reservoir and also on the road between the Boddingtons and on Welsh Road. Cross-field section unsuitable.

Refreshments: *The Carpenter's Arms* at Lower Boddington and *The Plough* at Upper Boddington serve meals lunchtime and evening (but not Sunday at *The Plough*). They both welcome children inside and each has a few outdoor tables for fine weather! The village stores at Upper Boddington can provide drinks, ice-creams, etc. but it is not open at weekends apart from on Saturday mornings.

Checklist – Score 2 points for each

1 A buoy
2 A *red* boat
3 A seagull
4 A pond (sharp eyes needed!)
5 Stables for horses
6 A well
7 A house with the name of a nut tree
8 A house with the name of a fruit tree
9 A hump-back bridge sign
10 A group of horse-chestnut trees
11 A bird table
12 A Telecom tower (a lesser version of the London one!)

Total Score _____

Your path around the reservoir

The Walk

⇒ From the car park at the north-east tip of the reservoir, cross the stile beside the metal gate at the end farthest from the road. Now continue on the broad gravelled track past the sailing club, after which the path becomes much narrower. Continue over the little wooden bridge, and afterwards swing to the right following the waymarked path around the reservoir's edge. Eventually cross the dam at its south end.

Q1   The red circular cases you can see on the dam contain life-belts. How many in all can you see? _____

Score 1 point for each.

Score ____

⇒ At the end of the dam, leave the reservoir and climb uphill to the wooden kissing gate ahead. Through the gate, cross the field going diagonally uphill to the right to where a tall tree stands on the skyline.

Q2   What sort of tree is this? _____

Score 2 points _____

☺ Just for the record, it is Northamptonshire's commonest tree, and there are several more in the hedge you will now follow to the road.

⇒ At the tree, turn left and take the broad grassy track beside the hedge to reach the road. Cross directly over the road and keep straight ahead in the field opposite. Leave the field by a stile and in the next field dip down to the bottom right-hand corner where a gate leads you on to a bridleway. Turn left on the bridleway to reach the road.

Q3   As you pass through the village of Lower Boddington, how many houses can you see whose names begin with 'The Old – – -", e.g. The Old Post Office?

Score 1 point for each.

Score _____

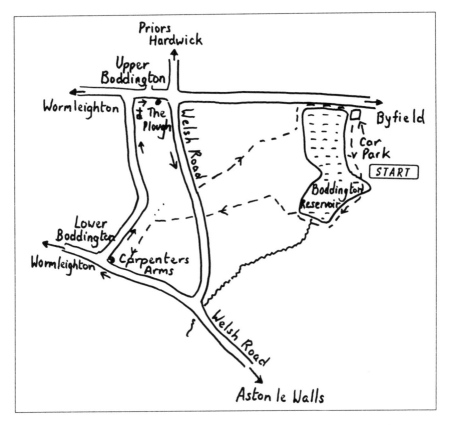

⇒ Turn right on the road and follow it to the junction at the *Carpenters Arms.* Turn right and keep to the road all the way to Upper Boddington.

☺ At the top of the hill there are fine views westwards across the Warwickshire plain. Can you see the gleaming roofs of the glass-houses at the nurseries just below you?

⇒ Walk through Upper Boddington past the church, the shop and the school to reach the road junction.

Q4   How many windows are there in the west wall of the church tower (the wall facing you)? _____

Score 2 points _____

⇒ Turn right at the road junction, and then right again just out of the village.

☺ You are now on 'Welsh Road', the route down which the drovers of Wales once brought their cattle to fetch better prices in the markets of London. It was a hard journey, which lasted several weeks – can you imagine it? You may have seen the recent BBC Television serial *Drovers' Gold* which told the story.

⇒ After approximately half a mile, turn left at the first bridleway sign. Cross the field heading diagonally left to a hedge corner at the top of the slope. Now walk downhill keeping the hedge on your left and continue into the next field with the hedge on your right. Keep to the path, at the bottom of the field bearing left around the perimeter to reach the road at a small car park beside the reservoir.

☺ There are many ancient hedgerows in this part of the world, and the one across the road running to the left is an excellent example. Field Maple and Dogwood are here, and so is the rare Midland Hawthorn. It looks just like an ordinary hawthorn, but if there are berries on the trees you can tell – the Midland Thorn has two seeds inside instead of the usual one. If you find it, give yourself a BONUS! (We can't really give you a score because there aren't always berries!)

⇒ From the small car park, steps lead up to the top of the reservoir wall. Walk along the top to its far end, cross the road bridge, and return along the short track to the car park.

Well done! Now let's look at the score ...

More than 25   Fantastic!

15 – 25   Pretty good try!

Under 15   What went wrong?

And if you have scored the bonus – *CONGRATULATIONS!*

Walk 11: Fawsley

Parkland and woods

Fawsley Park is delightful. In the extensive grounds of Fawsley Hall, a tiny grey church stands alone on a hill overlooking lakes and parkland landscaped by Capability Brown. You are free to wander beside the water and on the many footpaths which cross the park.

Fawsley Hall was once the home of the Knightley family. That little church, which is usually open, contains many memorials to them. But there is a sad story here. Once there was a village of Fawsley, with as many as 300 inhabitants. The Knightleys wished to become sheep farmers, and at the end of the 15th century, they turned out the villagers and enclosed the land for their flocks. The deserted village was drowned when the lakes were created some 250 years later. Sheep still graze the area to this day!

The walk takes you over the hill to Badby, often said to be the prettiest village in Northamptonshire. You can judge for yourselves! Here are two excellent old inns and a tiny village shop, which between them should be able to supply all your refreshment needs. The return route passes through Badby Wood, at the heart of which is a high point known as Hazley Knob. Children will love to play a while here – there are fallen trees to climb, and a fine view over all the woodland. The woods are famous for their bluebells – but many think the wood anemones, which come before them, are equally beautiful. So take this walk in springtime, if you want a real treat! When you leave the splendours of the wood, a short walk across the parkland brings you back to the lakeside – an ideal spot for a picnic!

Starting Point: Fawsley Park, Grid Ref. 565569. The park is 3 miles south of Daventry, and can be reached by turning where signed off the A361. It can also be reached from the unclassified road from Newnham to Preston Capes.

Parking: There are various pull-offs beside the road which runs through the park, particularly above the lake and at the sharp bend in the road.

Distance: 3½ miles

Map: O.S. Landranger 152, Northampton and Milton Keynes

Terrain: Well-marked grassy paths over hilly parkland. The paths in Badby woods can be muddy, particularly in winter.

Public Toilets: None

Pushchairs: Possible only on the road through the park.

Refreshments: There are two fine old pubs in Badby, *The Windmill* and *The Maltsters Arms*. Both cater very well for children, have a special children's menu and some outside eating area. *The Maltsters Arms* has a garden with bouncy castle. Badby also boasts a Post Office and Village Stores. There is lots of space for picnicking around the lake in Fawsley Park – and plenty of willing ducks and swans to share your meal!

Checklist – Score 2 points for each

1   A rabbit hole (try looking under a big tree!)
2   A telecommunications tower
3   Someone walking a brown dog (no, not just any dog!)
4   Two stone lion-heads
5   A hollow tree
6   A cartwheel
7   A Nene Way signpost
8   A squirrel
9   A brick archway leading into the wood (look all around – you don't actually walk through it!)
10   A weather vane on a golden ball
11   A lion-head door-knocker
12   A waterfall (you might hear it first!)

Total Score _____

Horse Chestnuts on the green at Badby

The Walk

⇒ Where the road through the park turns a sharp corner, not far from the gate leading to the church, a white disc on a pole beside a gate marks the route of the 'Knightley Way'. Go through that gate, and follow a series of these discs uphill through the parkland.

Q1   On the way uphill, you pass through what appears to be a very narrow field, with a row of trees planted on each side. It must, at one time, have been a long avenue. What sort of trees make the avenue?

_____

Score 3 points _____

☺ Nearing the top of the hill, you find yourself in a strange area where dead and dying trees appear in grotesque shapes. These trees are actually dying from old age — they are beech trees which were planted as saplings about 200 years ago.

⇒ At the top of the hill, still lead by the discs of the Knightley Way, cross a stile beside a metal gate and immediately turn right to enter Badby Woods. Follow the path downhill along the edge of the woods until eventually you reach a stile (with a white disc marker) leading out into a field. Cross the field to the bottom right-hand corner and, in the next field, look for a waymarked stile in the hedge on the left. This leads into a narrow lane, which eventually brings you out opposite the church at Badby.

☺ This beautiful old church dates from the 14th century. It overlooks a little green with an old horse-chestnut tree, and just down the lane is Northamptonshire's only Youth Hostel.

Q2   There are many old cottages in Badby — and some new ones which look old as well. Some have a date on them. For one point each, can you spot 1686, 1722 and 1966? _____

_____

Score ____

⇒ Turn right and walk down the hill to the little green.

Q3   Just a little farther on below the green is the Youth Hostel. What
      two symbols are used internationally for a Youth Hostel? _____

_____

Score 2 points _____

⇒ Now go back to the lower church gate and turn down Vicarage Hill. At the
bottom, turn right, and continue past *The Windmill* inn to the stores beside
the village green. If you wish to visit *The Maltsters Arms* it is just ahead of you
around the corner, but otherwise you should turn right here and go down
Chapel Lane. After crossing the brook — which soon joins another tributary to
become the River Nene — take the footpath signed at the top of the bank on
the right. Cross the field to the top right-hand corner, where two stiles lead
you through into another field. Head straight across this over the hill, and
before you lies the woodland edge. Directly ahead at the bottom of the field is
a piece of fence painted white, and this marks your point of entry into the
wood.

☺ The wood was once a deer park, but there aren't usually any deer here
   now. You could look out for squirrels though — and birds, too!

Q4   You can hear birds singing in the wood, but they aren't so easy to
      spot. How many *different* kinds of birds can you see while you are in
      the wood? Score 1 point for each one.

Score _____

⇒ On entering the wood, go straight ahead, and then bear right on a wide
track. Where this is joined by a track from the left, keep straight on and then
bear left, uphill, to reach Hazley Knob. This is the highest point of the wood
and it is easy to find — although it is not easy to describe the route through the
many woodland paths.

☺ It is a lovely spot to linger for a while, perhaps with a picnic.

⇒ When you are ready to leave, look for the track on which you came, and
stand on the Knob with this track behind you. Take the narrow track which
leads down the hill to the right. At the bottom of the hill this crosses a broad
track and continues, bearing right. Keep to this track for some distance.
Ahead of you, and uphill again, is the rim of the wood, and this is where you

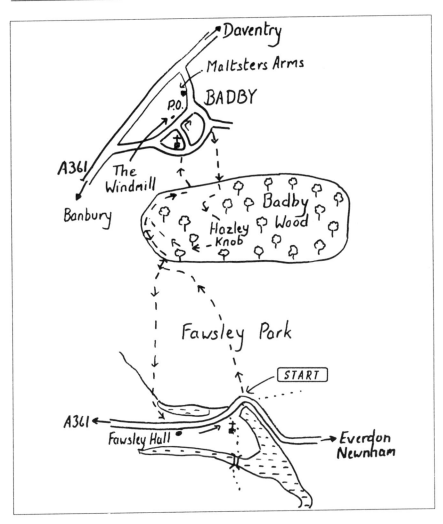

are finally going, reaching the track along the edge which you came along earlier. When you arrive at this track, turn left, and with the wood on your left, head uphill following the Knightley Way signs again.

⇒ Emerging from the wood, go through the metal gate on the left, as before, but now turn right, and, following waymarks, head downhill beside the hedge. Soon you come to another of those fine wooden gates and the route is well waymarked through the fields towards Fawsley Hall.

Q5   After you have left the wood, how many wooden gates do you go
     through before you reach the Hall? _____

Score 1 point for each.

Score _____

⇒ After the last wooden gate, follow the path around the hill and look for the
point where it crosses the brook on the right. Over the brook, turn
immediately left and slightly uphill to a squeeze stile in a fence. Cross the
next two fields on the obvious path to come out opposite Fawsley Hall. Turn
left on the road.

☺ The Hall is no longer owned by the Knightley family. It was used as an
    army base in the second World War and after that as a timber factory. It
    has since been divided into appartments and is now also a luxury hotel.

⇒ Walk along the road, and soon you will come to the gate leading to the
church. You are almost back at your car, but you really must visit it!

Q6   In front of the church is a sort of ditch with a wall at the back-
     curiously called a ha-ha! Why do you think the ha-ha was put here?
     _____

Score 4 points _____

☺ The church is usually open and you should be able to get inside. Look
    for the high pews in which the Knightley family sat – they didn't wish to
    be seen by the rest of the congregation! But of course, they couldn't see
    what was going on, so they had to have a hole in the wall to peep
    through! Look also at all the carvings on the pews. Can you find the owl
    and the pussy-cat? Well, they are not both together, but there is an owl,
    and there is a cat! If you can find them both, take a BONUS! There are
    also lots of monuments and brasses and priceless medieval stained
    glass windows – you can buy a booklet inside to tell you about them all.

⇒ Return to the road and walk to the right to reach your starting point.

Well done! And now it's score time again ...

More than 32   Sharp as a needle!

20 – 32   Still pretty sharp!

Under 20   Well, never mind!

And if you have scored the bonus – **CONGRATULATIONS!**

Walk 12: Flore

A watery walk by canal and river

The Grand Union Canal, the main artery of the inland waterways system, runs through the heart of Northamptonshire. On this walk we follow its winding course for 2 miles between the neighbouring villages of Flore and Nether Heyford. There is never a dull moment! The canal is alive with boats even in winter, and there are excellent views across the valley of the River Nene.

For the return, we keep to the Nene Way, a Long Distance Path which follows the route of the river from its source near Badby in the west to its mouth on The Wash in the east. The river is just100 miles long – the seventh-longest river in Britain! The section of the Nene Way we follow here takes us across low-lying fields beside the river, where sheep and cattle graze alongside drifting flocks of geese, and silent herons haunt the water's edge.

Both Flore and Nether Heyford are well worthy of exploration. Flore is a pretty village of winding streets and thatched cottages. You may well find visitors from across the Atlantic wandering here – it is the birthplace of the parents of John Adams, 2nd. President of the U.S.A., whose son, John Quincey Adams later became the sixth President. Nether Heyford is a more rambling village set around one of the largest village greens in the country – it covers 2 hectares in all. Both villages have friendly pubs, shops selling all you could possibly require for a snack or picnic, and good recreation areas suitable for children.

Starting Point: Brodie Lodge Playing Field, Spring Lane, Flore. Grid Ref. 644599. Flore is on the A45, 5 miles west of Northampton. The playing field is at the lower end of the village.

Parking: There is a small car park beside the playing field.

Distance: 4 miles

Map: O.S. Landranger 152, Northampton and Milton Keynes

Public Toilets: None

Pushchairs: Not suitable, apart from short section in the village of Nether Heyford.

Refreshments: The *Foresters Arms,* beside the green at Nether Heyford, serves meals every day except Sundays, and welcomes children both inside and out. Also at Nether Heyford, *The Olde Sun* (in Middle Street, on left at far end of green) serves meals every day (not Monday lunchtimes) and has a garden area as well as welcoming children inside. In Flore, *The White Hart* and *The Royal Oak* (on the main road, the A45) both usually serve meals at lunchtime, though it may be worth checking. Both welcome children. There are shops beside the green at Nether Heyford and on the A45 at Flore. If you have brought your own picnic, you will find pleasant seats on the green at Nether Heyford. If not, you could consider *The Heyford Patisserie* (at the corner of the green opposite Church Street) which serves excellent snacks including tea and coffee for taking away.

Checklist – for 2 points each

1   A horse
2   A heron
3   A flag
4   A boat with the name of a bird
5   A duck
6   A train
7   A cottage with the name of a fruit tree
8   A picture of a bicycle in a red circle
9   The date 1905
10 An old ruined water mill
11 A dog
12 A thatched wall

Total Score ____

The Walk

⇒ From the Playing Field car park, walk directly across the playing field to cross a stile in the opposite hedge. On the road, turn right and then almost immediately left at the road junction. Walk up the road for about half a kilometre, crossing two bridges over the River Nene. Just before the canal bridge, go through the gate on to the towpath and turn left under the bridge (the canal is now on your right)

☺ The Grand Union Canal runs from Paddington in west London to the heart of Birmingham. In the early 1800s it was an important trade route carrying all manner of commodities between the two cities. But its hey-day was not long! The railways took over and canal trade failed. Now the boats are all pleasure craft, but many of them try to keep the original working boats' design and decoration.

Q1 Traditional canal boats were painted with 'Roses and Castles' – very distinctive! As you walk along, can you spot any boats with traditional painting? (Roses or castles will do, although you will often see both together)

Score 3 points _____

☺ All the bridges have numbers and most of them have names, too. Bridge 28 has an interesting feature!

Q2 As you pass under the bridge, look for the black iron posts beside the edges of the brickwork. There are deep grooves in these. What do you think made the grooves?

_____

_____

Score 4 points _____

'Roses and Castles' decorated jug

☺ The canal may be for boats, but walkers use the towpath. The whole length of it between the two cities has been restored and is now used as a Long Distance Path – The Grand Union Canal Walk. At least you can't get lost while following a canal! But in case you go the wrong way, the marker posts tell you in which direction you are walking!

Q3 You will pass a Grand Union Canal Walk post on the towpath. Are you heading towards London or Birmingham? _____

Score 2 points _____

⇒ Continue on the towpath under Bridge 29 to the next bridge which is actually Bridge 32 (Yes, some have disappeared! You may have noticed the remains of Bridge 30, a swingbridge, beside the cottage on the wide curve) Leave the canal at Bridge 32 and turn left to walk down the road into Nether Heyford.

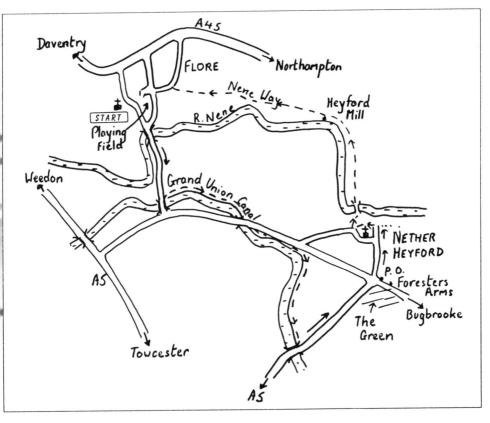

☺ The large village green is on your right. It is a pleasant area to play (there is play equipment at the far end) or to eat your lunch.

Q4 The huge trees around the edge of the green are rather unusual – at least, they are not oak or ash! What do you think they are? (If you don't know, you could try asking someone!) _____

Score 4 points ____

⇒ At the corner of the green, cross the road into Church Street. Go straight ahead and continue into Manor Walk. At the end of this cul-de-sac, go up some steps in the wall on your left and through the churchyard. You are now on the Nene Way.

☺ Churches are always interesting! In this one there is a brass of Sir Wal-
ter Mauntell and his wife from 1487. You will have to hunt for it though —
it is under the carpet to the left of the altar. Some people collect
'rubbings' of these old brasses. They cover the brass with a huge piece
of paper and rub wax over it to make the pattern come out — just as you
have probably done with a coin and a crayon. Would you like to try
brass-rubbing one day? You could make a fine decoration for the wall of
your room!

⇒ When you leave the church, continue along Church Lane and turn right at
the end of the wall, following the Nene Way sign. Continue on the path beside
the gardens of the houses and eventually cross the river on a metal bridge.
Now bear slightly left parallel to the river (ignore path going uphill to right).
Continue ahead on the Nene Way — it is clearly marked as it crosses the
fields.

Q5 You will now climb over many stiles on your way back to Flore. Try
counting them — how many do you cross on your way home after you
have left the metal bridge? (This is not so simple! There are so many
it is easy to lose count! Include the 'different' squeeze stile in your
total.) Total number of stiles crossed _____

Score 4 points for correct total, 3 points for nearly correct!

Score _____

⇒ At one point you pass the ruined Heyford Mill, now dangerous in its
tumbledown state. The route is quite obvious and well-marked, crossing
several fields before climbing slightly to reach the village of Flore.

Q6 Somewhere in the fields, just beside the path, is a White Willow tree,
bearing a plaque telling you it was planted in 1994. Who presented
the tree? _____

Score 2 points _____

⇒ Leave the final field through a kissing gate to enter a short path leading to a
lane.

On either side of this path are thatched walls – rather unusual! The walls are made of 'Wattle and Daub' – a sort of mud and straw or stick mixture, which needs the protection of thatch.

⇒ Continue ahead on the lane, ignoring all turnings on the right, to reach the playing field boundary with the entrance in Spring Lane.

Well done! And now are you ready for the score . . .

More than 30   Superb effort!

20 – 30   A good day's work!

Under 20   What happened?

Walk 13. Brixworth

Pitsford Water and the Brampton Valley Way

If you have never been to Brixworth Country Park, you will be surprised at
the treat that awaits! From its grassy slopes high above Pitsford Water, a
seemingly endless view of coves and inlets is laid before you; ducks dabble,
cormorants fish, and on a fine weekend, sails flash in the sunlight. Around
this southern end of the water is an 8-mile track for cyclists and walkers,
while beside the car park are picnic tables, an information centre and a cafeteria – all with a view!

This fascinating scene is the start of an equally fascinating walk. After
climbing away from the water, a long track leads to the Brampton Valley
Way, Northamptonshire's linear park which was once the route of the
Northampton to Market Harborough railway line. This is easy walking,
with good views in all directions and convenient seats for a picnic or snack.
The route continues across fields to Brixworth and past the famous Saxon
church. Interesting old houses line the roads and there are shops and inns
for refreshment. From the village, a footpath leads back to Pitsford Water
and a short walk on its perimeter track returns you to the car park.

Starting Point: Brixworth Country Park, Grid Ref.755695. From A508
Northampton – Market Harborough road, turn where signed, just south of
Brixworth.

Parking: There is ample parking at the Country Park.

Distance: 5½ miles.

Maps: O.S. Landranger 152, Northampton and Milton Keynes; O.S. Landranger
141, Kettering and Corby

Terrain: Hard surface on Brampton Valley Way. Some cross-field paths.

Public Toilets: At Brixworth Country Park.

Pushchairs: On Brampton Valley Way only.

Refreshments: The cafeteria at the Country Park is open every day and serves
light meals. There are several inns in Brixworth – *The Coach and Horses, The
George* and *The Red Lion* are all on the High Street. Only the first two serve food,
and both are welcoming to children and have outdoor eating areas. Brixworth
Country Park is well supplied with picnic tables – all with a view – should you
fancy an alfresco meal.

Extras to take: Binoculars – there are fine views over the water and on the walk.
Bicycles (although you can hire them on site) – just in case you should have en-
ergy left after the walk!

Checklist – for 2 points each

1   A tractor
2   A horse's hoof-prints
3   A sheep
4   2 acorns on a sign (the sign of the Midshires Way)
5   A fire station
6   The number 17 in large white painted figures
7   A bike drawn in red
8   The date 1811
9   An old-fashioned street lamp
10   A rabbit hole
11   A thatched house
12   A man-made pond (no, not Pitsford Water!)

Total Score _____

The Walk

⇒ Leave the Country Park via the access road and walk up to the roundabout. Cross the A508 with care, and take the road towards Brixworth. After about 400 metres, turn left on a track signposted to the Brampton Valley Way. Follow this track for almost 2km.

☺   This track is called Merry Tom Lane, and there is a story associated with it. A former Earl Spencer was riding his favourite hunter, Merry Tom, along the lane, when unfortunately the horse tripped and broke its neck. The Earl had the horse buried where it fell, and from that time the track became 'Merry Tom Lane'. It is still a bridleway today, and cannot be too dangerous as it is evidently very popular with horse-riders!

Q1   As you walk down Merry Tom Lane, you can see a bridge across fields on the right. The bridge is actually an old railway bridge on the Brampton Valley Way. How many arches has this bridge? (beware – it's a bit deceptive! You could check your answer when you cross over it later!)

Number of arches _____

For correct answer, score 4 points. Score _____

⇒ On reaching the Brampton Valley Way crossing, turn right, and follow the way for approximately 2½km to the car park on the Spratton road.

☺ The old railway line along here was closed in 1981, and 12 years later its route was re-opened as a linear park, 14 miles in length. It makes an exciting cycle ride – there are two long tunnels en route. As you can see, the track follows a small river – and crosses it twice. This is the River Brampton, which is usually called the Brampton Arm of the River Nene It joins the main river (which flows from the west) in the centre of Northampton.

☺ The sides of the track are a haven for wildlife of all kinds. Try counting how many different birds you see – although we cannot give you a score for it! And watch out for rabbits, whose burrows you can see in the banks.

Q2 As you walk along the track, you will see that seats have been carefully placed at points where the view is good. How many seats do you pass before you reach the car park at Spratton Crossing?

_____

Score 1 point for each.

Score ____

⇒ At Spratton road, turn right.

☺ The car park here is a very popular place. Picnic tables are provided in the grassy area alongside, and there are other picnic spots close by, as you will see from the signs.

Q3 What four symbols are carved on the post to show who may use the Brampton Valley Way? _____

_____

Score 4 points _____

⇒ About 50 metres along the road, a footpath on the left leads towards Brixworth Church. Follow this obvious path across the first field, and then

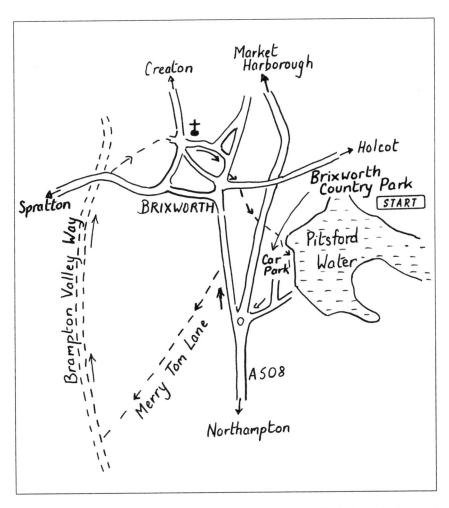

along the hedge in the second. Cross a stile, and then climb through the next field guided by the church spire.

Q4   What is on top of the church spire? _____

Score 2 points _____

⇒ Cross the next field, and then follow beside a stone wall to reach a gap with a stile. A short path and another stile now lead to a short drive, which in turn leads to the road. Do not turn left, but continue almost straight ahead where you can see a sign directing you to Brixworth Church.

☺ It is well worth walking up the short track to the church! People come from all over England — and beyond — to visit it, so you must see it while you are so close. It was built around 680, and is quite probably the oldest church in England. The Saxons who built it used any materials available to them, and you can straight away see the red Roman bricks set all higgledy-piggledy in the arches above the doors and windows. If you want to know more about the church, it is always open, so go inside. There are many guide books, and even special ones for children.

Roman brickwork in an arch at Brixworth church

☺ When you come down from the church, look across the road where an ancient and broken butter-cross stands on the green.

Q5   What is on the green behind the butter-cross, and what was its use?

_____

Score 3 points _____

⇒ At the road junction, turn right along the High Street. Opposite the third inn (The George), a short lane beside the parish hall leads you up to the Holcot Road. Here turn left, and in about 200 metres look for a very well-concealed narrow path on the right (just after Holdenby Designs). This leads you ahead through new housing estates where the streets have very curious names!

Maintaining the same direction, you are eventually led down a path which crosses over the A 508. It then leads down beside the hedge to the track around Pitsford Water. Here you turn right and wend your way over the hill to your starting point.

Well done! And now to check your score . . .

More than 30   Quite remarkable!

20 – 30   Pretty good!

Under 20   Not so hot today!

Walk 14. West Haddon

Rolling pastures, a lovely village, and a view

West Haddon has a pleasant playing field, and beside it, an even more pleasant pocket park. Here you can find a rustic playing area for children, with picnic tables alongside – an excellent place to start and finish your walk. And if you prefer your meal prepared for you, there are three pubs in the village that welcome children.

From West Haddon, it is just a short walk across the fields to the little hamlet of Winwick. And what a pretty place it is – a white thatched cottage, a brick arched bridge and a little stream with flower-clad banks along its main street. Leaving this scene, you will pass Victorian Winwick Hall and come to an attractive pond with a bench beside, yet another place for an alfresco snack!

From here, your route leads on to a high point with fine views to the west, which you can then enjoy as you cross the rolling fields to return to West Haddon.

Starting Point: West Haddon Playing Field, Grid Ref. 634717. West Haddon lies on the A428 Northampton – Rugby road, 10 miles north of Northampton. It can also be reached from the A14 via Cold Ashby.

Parking: There is parking alongside the playing field (near the entrance and by the pavilion), which can be found on the A428, just south-east of the village.

Distance: 4 miles

Map: O.S. Landranger 140, Leicester and Coventry

Terrain: Cross-field paths and track.

Public Toilets: None

Pushchairs: Not suitable

Refreshments: There are three pubs in West Haddon, *The Crown, The Pytchley Inn,* and *The Sheaf*. Only the latter two serve meals, *The Sheaf* welcoming children at lunchtime only. *The Pytchley Inn* has a children's menu available at all times, and also has a beer garden.

Checklist – for 2 points each

1   A man with a chef's hat on!
2   A rabbit
3   A tractor
4   A waterfall (an artificial one)
5   A marshy area with sedges
6   A black post box (instead of red!)
7   Sheep's wool on a barbed wire fence
8   A house with a clock above its door
9   A weather vane with a man ploughing
10   A cat
11   Watercress – the bright green leafy plant that grows in clean streams
12   A sign saying 'Public Footpath to West Haddon'

Total Score _____

The Walk

⇒ From the Playing Field, walk past the pavilion and downhill, passing the playground on your right. A short path now leads you out to the road, where you turn right.

Q1   First of all, something to look out for! On this walk you will pass two old water pumps, and in one place, just the remains of a pump with the trough below. Look out for them, and score 2 points for each!

Score _____

Q2   Something else to look out for – a fire insurance badge. But here we will give you a clue! It is on a house that you pass in the village of West Haddon. Years ago, when a house had taken out fire insurance, it was issued with a plaque to fix on the wall. There were many different companies, and many different plaques. The one you are looking for here is in the shape of a sun with long rays and a smiling face in the centre. What was the name of the house on which you saw it? _____

Score 3 points ____

⇛ At the road junction, turn left. Just before the *Crown Inn* on the opposite side of the road, turn right up Crown Lane. At the top of the path, a kissing gate leads you into a field. You are now on the Jurassic Way and will follow it through to Winwick. In this first field, keep straight ahead to the top, ignoring the waymarked gate on the left. Continue with the hedge on your left. Cross the next big field directly, and in the next field, bear left through a hedge to join the track. Keep on this briefly, and then cross a field to go through a waymarked white gate on the right. Keep ahead on the lane into Winwick.

Main street in Winwick

Q3   Soon you will pass Winwick Mill. There is a small stream flowing alongside the road, which is crossed at intervals by pipes to the houses. Between Winwick Mill and the brick bridge in the village, how many pipes cross the stream? Score 1 point for each pipe.

Score _____

Q4   At the road junction is a bus shelter. What does it commemorate?

_____

Score 2 points _____

⇒ Turn right at the junction beside the white cottage and walk uphill. (But go straight ahead if you wish to see the 13th century church and Elizabethan Manor House)

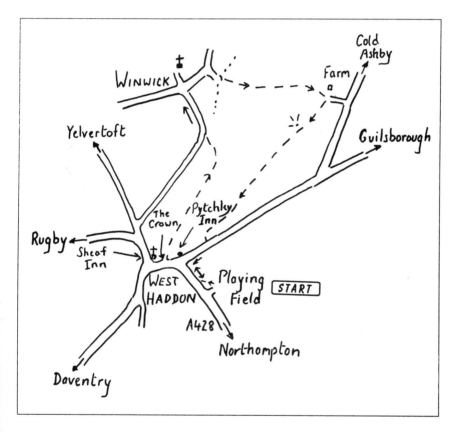

Q5   The red post box in the wall is quite old. Who was on the throne when it was made? _____

Score 2 points _____

Q6   Before you get back to the playing field, work this one out. You will
     pass Winwick Hall, and later you will pass a Baptist Chapel. Which
     was built first, and by how many years? _____

Score 4 points _____

⇒ At the pretty pond bear right, and at the end of the lane go through a gate
on the left. Turn right immediately on to an obvious field track, now leaving
the Jurassic Way which goes straight ahead here. Keep to this grassy track,
going uphill, down across the brook, and uphill again. At the top of the hill,
with White House Farm on the left, go through a gate and turn sharp right.

☺ There are fine views to the right across Leicestershire to the north and
Warwickshire to the west. The masts of Rugby radio station are clearly
seen.

⇒ Follow the waymarkers straight across two fields and slightly to the right
downhill across the next two. Now walk uphill, keeping just right of the
corrugated iron barn. Through the gate beside this, turn right across the
stream on a waymarked plank bridge. In the next big field, keep the hedge on
your right all the way across, ignoring the path going off to the left before the
brick building. There is a gap in the wire fencing before the housing estate,
and here you turn left to reach the road. Turn right and follow the road to the
junction you passed earlier, where now a left turn will return you to the playing
field.

Well done! Now add up your score . . .

More than 36   Top of the class!

20 – 36   A good pair of eyes!

Under 20   Try another walk – practice makes perfect!

Walk 15. Barby

Old villages and ancient pastures

On the county's boundary with Warwickshire, Barby and Kilsby are two attractive villages separated by gently rolling pastures divided by little streams. This is the last of the high ground before the Warwickshire plain, and there are excellent views. Many of the fields show the ridge-and-furrow effect of medieval farming and have not come under the plough since that time.

Your starting point is beside the pretty church and little playing field at Barby. It is just a short stroll from here across the fields to Kilsby, and once there, a delightful pub with an exciting children's playground can provide you with lunch. Alternatively, you could have a picnic beside the playing field in the village. Kilsby has a wealth of interesting streets to explore before you set out again.

Your return gives you the best of the views, and you can see Rugby to the north-west, and the ventilation shafts of Kilsby railway tunnel away on the hill to the east. This is just a short walk to be enjoyed on a clear day!

Starting Point: Barby village, Grid Ref. 543703. Barby can be reached by taking a (signed) unclassified road west from the A361 north of Daventry, or through Kilsby.

Parking: Cars may park in the Village Hall car park beside the church, on Kilsby Road at the south end of the village. Should the car park be full when there is a function, roadside parking is possible.

Distance: 3 miles

Maps: O.S. Landranger 140, Leicester and Coventry; O.S. Landranger 152, Northampton and Milton Keynes

Terrain: Cross-field paths and pavements in villages. Short road section.

Public Toilets: None

Pushchairs: Only in the villages

Refreshments: *The Arnold Arms* in Barby welcomes children and has an outside eating area with playground. *The Red Lion* in Kilsby (Main Street) caters well for children with special menu and interesting play equipment. There are village stores in both Barby (at The Green on Rugby Road) and Kilsby (in Independent Street). Each village has a pleasant playing field with benches where you could take a picnic.

Checklist – for 2 points each

1   A 'Ridge and Furrow' field
2   The masts of a radio station
3   A tunnel ventilation shaft (look in the distance!)
4   A green seat
5   A brown sheep (well, there are lots of white ones!)
6   A white gate
7   A half-circle window
8   A house with the name of a month
9   A cottage where Santa Claus might live!
10 A notice telling owners to keep dogs on a lead
11 A water tower
12 A pond in a field

Total Score _____

Playing field at Barby

The Walk

⇒ Leaving the Village Hall car park, turn left, and then take the first road on the right (Star Corner). Where this road forks, keep to the left and find the footpath between houses 11 and 15. (What happened to 13? The builder of this road must have been very superstitious!) This footpath runs beside gardens and then crosses the brook, after which you turn left across the field.

☺ You will see that the fields here show 'ridge and furrow', as do many you will see later. When the fields were divided into strips in medieval times, the plough, turning the soil always inward, caused the centre of the strip to be raised, while the edges sank.

Q1   You will cross lots of stiles today – it certainly wouldn't be easy to count them all! But give yourself 1 point for every 3 stiles you cross and keep a tally as you go!

Score _____

⇒ Cross four small fields in succession before reaching a much larger field. Head across this one to the bottom left-hand corner where a bridge takes you across the brook. The route is waymarked all the way. In the next large field, you walk downhill to the brook which you cross just before taking the track under the M45. In the next field, bear right uphill to a stile near the top right-hand corner. Turn right on the road into Kilsby.

☺ Kilsby must have been a quiet, sleepy village until first the canal to the west and then the railway to the east were built. A tunnel was needed to take the railway through the hill behind Kilsby – you can still see the huge ventilation shafts.

Q2   Devon Ox Road seems a curious name. Can you guess where it might have come from? _____

Score 2 points _____

⇒ At the junction, cross the main road following signs to the 'Village only'. Continue up Manor Road passing the school and the path to the church on your right.

Q3   In Kilsby there are still several 'wattle and daub' walls. These old
     walls were made from mud and twigs or straw and usually had a
     thatched top to keep the rain from washing the mud away! The
     thatch today has often been replaced by tiles or corrugated roofing.
     As you walk through the village, look out for these walls — you will
     have to keep your eyes peeled as they are not quite on your route!
     But you can certainly see them, and if you do -

Score 4 points _____

⇒ Continue around the left-hand bend to come to a road junction with the
village stores opposite. Turn left here (Independent Street) and return to the
main road. Cross it, and then cross Barby Road into Ashby Road (but if you
wish to find the Red Lion, turn right down Main Road instead). Heading up
Ashby Road, take the second turning on the right, Arnills Way. At the end of
this, a footbridge will cross you over the M45.

☺ Don't forget to keep counting those stiles!

⇒ Head down the field, over the brook, and ahead following the waymarks.
Soon you pass through a small wooded area and emerge on a field. Cross in
the direction indicated and then head across the next field aiming for the
finger-post to the left of the barns at the top right-hand corner. Turn right on
the road.

☺ As you walk along this road you have excellent views to the north.

⇒ In about 400 metres, take the first footpath on the right, sign-posted to
Barby.

Q4   What tree is growing in the hedge to the left of the stile here?

_____

Score 2 points _____

⇒ Head across this field, aiming left of Barby Church. Over the stile, cross
the corner of the next field to another stile (still counting?). In the next field,
bear left to a gateway with waymarks. Turn right here, and with the hedge on
your left, head downhill. Keep straight on down, cross one stile, and then find
the stile on the left which you crossed at the start of your walk. Cross this

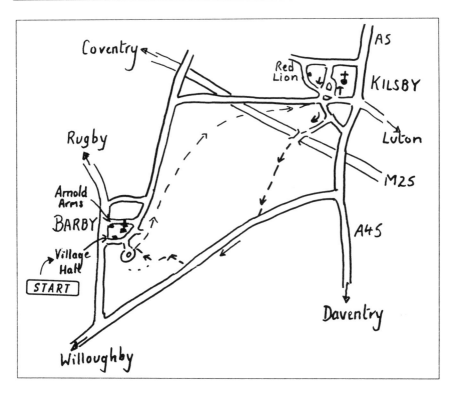

again now, and follow the path up beside the gardens and down the road to return to the Village Hall. But just before you get there – go down the path to the church. There's always something interesting to see in a church!

Q5 What interesting features can you see just below the top of the tower? (Aren't they lifelike?) _____

Score 4 points _____

Well done! And now for your score . . .

More than 30   Eagle-eyed!

20 – 30   Pretty sharp!

Under 20   You were asleep!

Walk 16. Welford

Water, water everywhere!

There is certainly a lot of water around Welford: your walk starts beside the canal, crosses a causeway between two reservoirs and meanders home alongside the River Avon. And there are other delights! After leaving the reservoirs, the path crosses the site of the Deserted Medieval Village of Sulby. This is particularly well preserved and you can clearly see the roads, or hollow-ways between the platforms where the houses stood. The village was abandoned around 1400, when the land was made over to sheep farming. There are still sheep here today!

Continuing over the pastures, you arrive at the village of Sibbertoft. This is set on high ground, and has more watery connections. The River Welland was said to rise in the cellar of the Old Rectory here, which has been demolished. There are, however, many other springs in the village contributing to the source of this river, which flows away to the north to form the boundary with Leicestershire. A friendly pub in the village can offer you refreshment.

On your return route, you cross pasture and woodland before coming on the site of the former Sulby Abbey. Once again an impressive array of hillocks and hollows gives you a feel for what once might have been! From here, you wander alongside the infant River Avon (the one that later flows through Stratford) towards distant Welford across the fields. But keep your ears open! It is said that a secret passage links Sulby Abbey with Welford Church, which you can see on the horizon. No-one has found that passage (you could try, of course!), but while crossing these fields some have heard ghostly noises, thought to be coming from the tunnel beneath!

Starting Point: Welford Wharf, Grid Ref. 644808. Welford lies on the A5199, 2 miles north of its junction with the A14. The Wharf is at the north end of the village, on the road to Husbands Bosworth.

Parking: at the wharf. Turn left off the road immediately after the *Wharf Inn*. If full, there is a small car park on the Naseby road, below the reservoir.

Distance: 6 miles

Maps: O.S. Landranger 140, Leicester and Coventry; O.S. Landranger 141, Kettering and Corby

Terrain: Cross-field paths and pavements in villages.

Public Toilets: At the Wharf.

Pushchairs: Not suitable

Refreshments: Besides the *Wharf Inn*, Welford boasts two other pubs serving meals and welcoming children. *The Shoulder of Mutton* (which serves special children's meals) and *The Elizabethan Restaurant* are both to be found in the High Street. *The Red Lion* at Sibbertoft serves children and has an outside eating area. For picnic needs, there is a Post Office and Stores on Welford High Street.

Checklist – A specially long one for a long walk!
For 2 points each . . .

1   A deserted village

2   A pond *with an island in the middle*

3   A rabbit

4   A squirrel

5   A glider!

6   A house with the name of an apple

7   A dovecote

8   An air-raid shelter

9   A horse

10   A horse-shoe

11   An electric fence

12   A greenhouse

13   A ruined brick corner in a field

14   A picture of a swan

15   A four-way wooden signpost where footpaths cross

Total Score _____

The Walk

⇒ From the main road at the wharf, turn right towards Welford and cross the bridge into Northamptonshire. At the junction, take the Naseby road. A short distance along, beside the car park, a Jurassic Way sign points you to the left. Follow the Way beside Welford Reservoir, and then over the causeway between the two reservoirs.

☺ The reservoir on your right is Sulby Reservoir. It was built nearly 200 years ago, and has an unfortunate story attached to it. When it was almost finished, a thaw caused its banks to burst and the water poured out into the River Avon below. The sudden flood drowned two people in

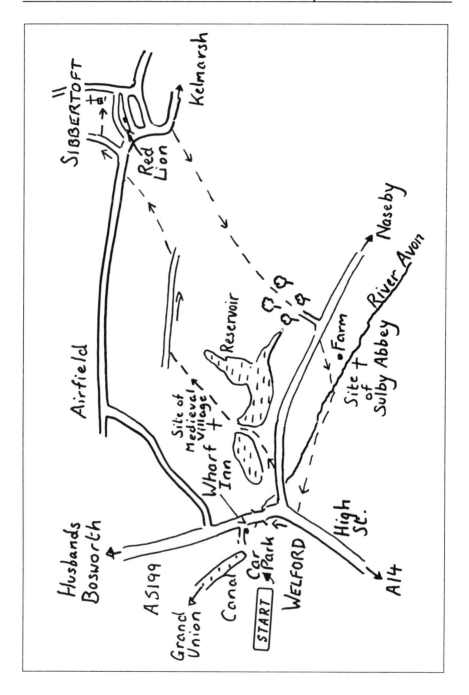

nearby Stanford. Both reservoirs, and the one at Naseby, were built to supply the canal system.

Q1 The reservoir is home for a variety of waterfowl – mallards, grebes, tufted duck, various geese and others. How many different species of birds can you see on the water? Score 1 point for each.

Score _____

Q2 How deep is the water in Sulby Reservoir today? _____

Score 2 points _____

Q3 This walk passes through many fields which provide grazing for sheep. For the duration of the walk, score 1 point for every stone drinking trough that you see.

Score _____

⇒ After the reservoirs, cross the stile and follow the Jurassic Way signs straight ahead up the field. After a stile, a plank bridge and a kissing gate, you enter the field which is the site of the medieval village of Sulby.

☺ The village is best seen in the long rays of early morning or late evening sunshine, when all the undulations seem exaggerated. But at any time you can easily see where the roads were – these are the sunken channels we call hollow-ways. You will cross two or three of them. Beside them you can make out rectangular areas which were the bases of the houses.

⇒ Continue over the ladder stile and into the next field.

Q4 A waymarker is fastened to an old and broken tree in the middle of this field. What sort of tree is it? _____

Score 2 points _____

⇒ After the field, cross the road and follow the Jurassic Way markers across the next field to a stile at the top right-hand corner. Turn right on the lane.

The area you are now passing through was an airfield and camp in the Second World War. Part of the airfield to the north is still used by a gliding club.

⇒ Continue on the lane to a metal gate with a kissing gate beside it. Here, follow the Jurassic Way signs across the field to the left. Past the spinney, a stile leads you into another field which you cross to the top left-hand corner. The waymarks now direct you between fields and then across two fields to reach the road at Sibbertoft. Turn right on the road and, at the first junction, bear left up Westhorpe. Just before the bungalows, a Jurassic Way sign leads you across two fields on the right to enter the churchyard.

Across the field to Sibbertoft church

Q5   To whom is this church dedicated? _____

Score 3 points _____

⇒ On emerging from the churchyard, turn right and shortly, right again down Welland Rise, and past the *Red Lion*. Turn left on the footpath which runs around the field at the bottom of Welland Rise.

☺ Many of the houses in Sibbertoft have springs rising beneath them or in their grounds. One of these springs can be seen in the field on your left – you can see the sunken brickwork where it rises.

⇒ At the end of the footpath continue along Naseby Road, and then at the road junction turn right, heading away from the village. Just after the road bends left, take the track on the right. This track bends right, then left, after which you go through a gap in the hedge on a bridleway which now runs beside a deep ditch.

☺ Don't forget to keep looking for stone troughs!

⇒ Where the ditch turns left, go straight ahead across the corner of a field, following the waymarks. The bridleway now goes across two more large fields, and at the bottom of the second one, turns right along the hedge. You now enter a sort of lane, and where this swings right, you should go through a metal gate on the left and cross the field to a gap in the woodland edge. Continue through the wood to a track, which emerges on the road. Turn right, and take the footpath signed on the left after about 100 metres.

☺ Ahead of you is the valley of the River Avon and behind it, Honey Hill which does not look so steep from this side.

Q6 What feature can you see on the top of Honey Hill? _____

Score 2 points ____

⇒ This footpath leads you downhill to cross the farm track and continue through a metal gate.

☺ As you go, you have a fine view of the site of Sulby Abbey. All those bumps and dips behind the farm are where it once stood. As you walk through the valley, you must be close to the line of that supposed secret passage. Can you hear anything? (There is no bonus for this!)

⇒ The waymarkers direct you to cross a bridge. On the far side, turn right and take the footpath beside the river. After two fields, you come to a watery junction where the feeder from Naseby Reservoir to the canal comes in from the left. It is difficult to work out what is going where here! But you should go through the gate into the next field and walk along the top with the hedge on your left. Cross the next field to the middle of the opposite hedge and follow the direction of the marker to Welford. Cross the next field to a stile close to the river.

⇒ Cross this field to a stile near the houses. This takes you along the edge of a garden, beside a red brick wall, and you get the feeling you shouldn't be here! But this is the route of the footpath, and soon you come to the front of a house where you need to go through the gate on to the road. Turn right, and then left at the junction to return to the wharf.

Very well done indeed! That was a really long walk! And now let's look at your score . . .

More than 36   Stupendous!

24 – 36   You kept your wits about you!

Under 24   You must be exhausted!

Walk 17: Arthingworth

A tunnel trek with torches!

The Brampton Valley Way is an odd-shaped park – 14 miles long and just a few yards wide, it is a long ribbon threading itself through the heart of the county. Once the route of the Northampton to Market Harborough railway, Northamptonshire County Council have taken it over and created here a park which is a fine area for recreation, while maintaining the banks as a natural habitat for wildlife of all kinds. The trackbed is hard-surfaced for walking and cycling, picnic areas are provided and seats are sited at viewpoints along the way. Also on the route are two tunnels, preserved as they were when the trains ran through. This walk will take you through one of them, and it is quite an adventure – you should certainly take torches to light your way!

Emerging on the far side of the tunnel, your route home takes you over the hill above. This is the highest point for miles around with excellent views in all directions. Continuing through the hilltop village of Arthingworth, you have the opportunity to visit the friendly *Bull's Head* inn before returning to your starting point, the picnic site at Kelmarsh station.

And for those who enjoyed their underground adventure, just a short walk along the line in the opposite direction will reveal the second tunnel for you to explore!

Starting Point: Picnic site at Kelmarsh Station, Grid Ref. 746804. From the A508, take the turning to Arthingworth, just north of Kelmarsh. The station area is just under the railway bridge on the left-hand side.

Parking: There is a car park beside the road, while the picnic tables are sited in a field behind the car park.

Distance: 4½ miles

Map: O.S. Landranger 141, Kettering and Corby.

Terrain: Hard-surfaced track along Brampton Valley Way, then field paths and short section on quiet road.

Public Toilets: None

Pushchairs: Only on the Brampton Valley Way and return route from Arthingworth.

Refreshments: *The George* is on the A508 at Great Oxendon, shortly after you emerge from the tunnel. They welcome children and do 'half-portions of every meal'. They also have an outside eating area. *The Bull's Head* at Arthingworth offers a children's menu and likewise has outdoor eating space. There are picnic tables at Kelmarsh Sation where this walk begins.

Extras to take: Torches! Although you can see from one end of the tunnel to the other, in the middle it is quite dark, and it is difficult to see the ground at your feet! The views are good, so binoculars could be useful.

Checklist – Score 2 points for each

1   A cyclist
2   A 'Ridge and Furrow' field (if you don't know what it is, see the Castle Ashby Walk)
3   A rabbit
4   A round window
5   A ventilation shaft
6   A house with a colour in its name
7   A wishing well
8   A pair of horns on a wall
9   A yellow post bearing the number 15
10   A hay bale
11   A church spire
12   A greenhouse

Total Score: _____

The Walk

⇒ From the car park, climb the steps to join the Brampton Valley Way. Turn right at the top on the track, and keep to it for about 3km to the tunnel entrance.

Q1   Lots of seats have been provided for you to take a rest! How many seats do you pass along the Brampton Valley Way today? _____

Score 1 point for each seat. Score _____

Q2   Behind a high-backed seat is a strange-shaped meadow. What shape is it? _____

Score 2 points _____

Q3   Soon you will pass a pond on the right. What creatures are being encouraged to come and live here? (You may need to do a little detective work!) _____

Score 4 points _____

⇒ Soon you will come to a road crossing where the faint-hearted are offered an alternative route avoiding the tunnel. But, of course, you won't take it! (If you do, it leads up beside the main road to Great Oxendon, where you can re-join this route on the Braybrooke Road). Continue ahead to the tunnel mouth.

Q4   How long is this tunnel? (It might feel a bit longer!) _____

Score 2 points _____

☺   Do try out the echo while you are going through! It will terrify anyone else in the tunnel! And if you really enjoy testing your nerves in the darkness, there's another tunnel you can try quite close to the car park you started from!

⇒ Once through the tunnel, climb the bank to the left before the bridge, following the Macmillan Way signs. This doubles back above the track along the bank. Do not swing left to cross the tunnel entrance, but turn right over a stile and then cross the field behind, heading uphill. Cross the next small field and then go right on the track to reach the A508. Turn left on the pavement and walk past *The George* to Braybrooke Road, where you again turn left. A footpath sign on the right before the garage (the last building) directs you across a field, keeping to the right of the tunnel ventilation shaft.

☺ The fields at the top of this hill have 'Open Access' under an agreement with the Countryside Commission. They show beautifully the 'ridge and furrow' effects of medieval farming. There is also a superb view from the top. The Brampton valley stretches before you, with Arthingworth on its hill, and Market Harborough away to the left.

⇒ Now that you can see Arthingworth, you will have no difficulty picking out your path over the several fields which lie in front of you. In any case, the route is quite well used, and leads from one gap in a hedge to the next until you cross a small bridge to reach the final field. Head straight across it towards the houses.

☺ Wandering through Arthingworth, you might well wonder what happened to all the old houses. Everything seems modern. This is not quite true, as you will see in a minute, but it is thought that the old cottages of Arthingworth were very poor and so did not survive.

Q5   There are three old farms in Arthingworth. For 2 points each, what are their names? _____

Score _____

⇒ When you come to the road junction, turn right towards Kelmarsh.

☺ When you leave Arthingworth, you cross a bridge over a small river. This is the Ise Brook which later flows through Kettering to join the River Nene in Wellingborough.

⇒ Keep to this road for half a mile to return to Kelmarsh Station.

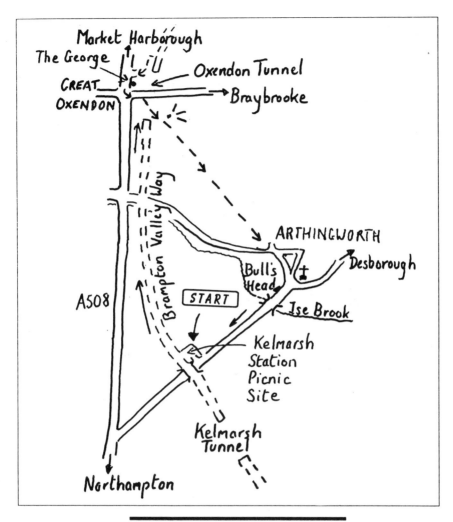

Well done! It's time again for that score . . .

More than 30 Absolutely fantastic!

20 – 30 A good attempt!

Under 20 Were you blindfolded?

Walk 18: East Carlton

A wander on the edge of the Welland

East Carlton Countryside Park is a park with a view! It is also a park with many winding woodland paths and nature trails, and some of the largest and oldest lime trees in England. Add to this a play area, an outdoor exhibition, craft workshops, a cafeteria and a heritage centre where the fascinating history of steel making is displayed, and you have easily a full day's entertainment for the whole family.

East Carlton Hall, at the centre of the park, was built by the Palmer family in 1873. It seems more like an old French chateau than an English country house! It is no longer lived in – at least, not by people, although it does have a resident ghost!

With all this waiting when you return, the walk described here is just a short one – enough for you to visit the attractive nearby villages of Middleton and Cottingham and take in the distant views from the hillside between them. Both villages have pubs happy to cater for children, and Cottingham also has a village shop. Your return takes you through *The Dale*, Cottingham's curious little pocket park, with its beautiful mature trees and a little stream that disappears underground.

Starting Point: East Carlton Countryside Park, Grid Ref. 835895. The Park is signposted from the A427 Corby – Market Harborough road, 3 miles west of Corby.

Parking: There is plenty of parking space in the grounds of the park.

Distance: 3 miles

Map: Landranger 141, Kettering and Corby

Terrain: Field paths and pavements through the villages.

Public Toilets: In East Carlton Countryside Park

Pushchairs: There are plenty of paths suitable for pushchairs in the park. The route outside the park is not suitable.

Refreshments: *The Red Lion* at Middleton, *The Spread Eagle* at Cottingham, and *The Royal George* at Cottingham are all on the route and all welcome children. Between them, you should be able to get a meal any lunchtime or evening. The Post Office at Cottingham can provide for picnic needs or snacks. The cafeteria at the Countryside Park is open every day, and serves light meals. There are plenty of picnic tables outside, should the weather be suitable.

Checklist – Score 2 points for each

1   A holly tree
2   A clock
3   A 'Ridge and Furrow' field
4   A cottage with the name of a tree
5   A cottage with the name of a flower
6   A boundary marker
7   A sheep
8   A wishing well (Yes, you can count the one in the park. But if you spot another one on your travels, you are very sharp-eyed! Earn yourself an extra 3 points!)
9   A water pump (Again, take an extra 3 points if you spot two of them!)
10   A squirrel
11   A lane 'that cannot see'
12   A spring

Total Score _____

Remnants of the steel industry in the Countryside Park

The Walk

⇒ Go out through the main gate of the park and turn right on the road.

☺ Opposite you, just to the left across the road, is a row of almshouses. These were given in 1668 by the Palmer family, the big landowners of the area. (They later made their fortune in biscuits – you may recognise the name!)

⇒ Continue to walk beside the grey stone wall until you reach a stile where a sign directs the Jurassic Way across the field on your right.

Q1   What is the name of the bungalow opposite the stile? _____
_____

Score 2 points _____

☺ This seems a strange name, but looking around you will soon see the reason behind it. One of the springs feeds a water trough in the field you are about to cross.

⇒ Follow the obvious path across the field and then along the lower boundary of the park.

☺ On your left you can see across the River Welland, which here is the boundary with Leicestershire. On the top of a little hill just across the river is the village of Bringhurst. It stands on the site of an original Saxon settlement dating from the 6th century. Those Saxons would have felt save with their commanding view of the valley!

Q2   As you walk, you will see lots of church spires across the river. You will have to keep your eyes open all the way to Middleton as different ones can be seen at different times! Score 1 point for each spire you see.

Score _____

⇒ The path continues in a straight line and eventually comes out on the road at the bottom of Middleton Hill.

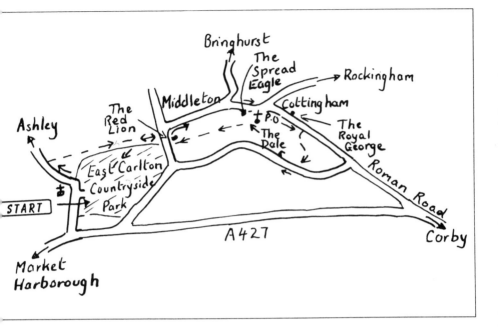

Q3 There are lots of dates scattered around Middleton. Before you reach the boundary with Cottingham, see if you can find 1862, 1992, 1868 (and you will have to be quick off the mark with this one!). Score 1 point for each.

Score _____

⇒ Turn left here and follow the road around the corner to the right. Walk right through the village with its lovely stone houses and into Cottingham (look for the boundary stone between the two). At the road junction, turn right and climb the hill past *The Hunting Lodge* to reach the village square at the top.

⇒ From the square, take the road signed to Corby. This road is actually part of the route of an old Roman Road, whose unswerving direction can be clearly seen on a map. When you reach Middlefield at the top of the hill, you will see a footpath sign on the opposite side of the road. Follow this path across three small fields, to leave the third at the top right-hand corner.

☺ Look at the fields as you cross – they show the 'ridge and furrow' effect caused by ploughing in the days before land was enclosed. The land was owned in strips, and the plough turning the earth always inwards caused the ridges.

⇒ Crossing a fourth field (with the hedge on your right) brings you out to the road. Now turn right, and in 50 metres take the footpath on the right. You are now at the top of The Dale.

☺ The Dale is a splendid little Pocket Park. The land seems to have been scooped out to give a rounded valley. The sides of the valley are limestone and in Spring and Summer there are lovely flowers. A small spring arises in this enchanted place, and after wet weather is joined by water running down the sides to be collected into a stream at the bottom. The stream then promptly disappears down a hole — which fortunately has been fenced in so that you can't disappear, too! It's an attractive spot for a picnic!

Q4 Some trees have been more recently planted at the higher end of The Dale (they are the same as the big tree on your left as you came in). What sort of trees are these? _____

Score 2 points _____

⇒ Leaving The Dale by the gate at the bottom, turn left on the path and continue keeping the fence on the right. You are now following the Jurassic Way back to Middleton.

☺ From this path, there are splendid views across the roof tops of Cottingham and Middleton to the scattered villages of the Welland Valley beyond.

⇒ The path comes out on a gravelly lane which you follow to the T-junction.

☺ At the junction is a fine old water pump, once used to supply water to these houses on the hill. It must have been hard work moving that huge handle!

⇒ Turn right down School Hill and continue to the bottom.

☺ Imagine going to school up this hill on a snowy wintery day!

Q5   When you reach Main Street at the bottom, glance up to the left. In the wall opposite is an old stone horse trough, again fed by a spring. What are the initials of the man who gave this trough in 1844?

_____

Score 2 points _____

⇒ Now turn right down the road and go back through the gate you used earlier. Follow again the long straight path to return to East Carlton Countryside Park (you could check on those spires on the way back!). But this time, turn left into the park through the first gate you reach (the one with the big signboard nearby)

⇒ Go uphill on the path, bearing right at the junction (towards the house). At the fork, again bear right, keeping below the house.

☺   The path crosses between two ponds where ducks play happily. There should be various sorts of white domesticated ducks and wild mallards, as well as moorhens and perhaps others.

Q6   Can you identify a male mallard? He should have a shiny green head with a yellow ring around his neck. (His poor wife is only dull brown!) If you see him, score 2 points.

Score _____

⇒ Continue on this path to return to the Heritage Centre.

_____

Well done! Have you made a big score? . . .

More than 30   Remarkable!

20 – 30   Good observation!

Under 20   Did you keep your eyes shut?

Walk 19: Wakerley

A woodland walk with a view!

Wakerley Great Wood and its neighbour, Fineshade, are the largest remaining tracts of the ancient Rockingham Forest which once covered this part of the county. In the Middle Ages, Rockingham Forest was maintained as a playground for royalty, a place where they could come and hunt the deer. Today, this is a working forest, but it is also a 'playground' for everyone. Here there are clearings with picnic tables and barbecues, two waymarked trails to lead you through the forest, and a permanent orienteering course. There are also endless miles of other woodland paths for you to explore.

The walk suggested here is one with a difference – it is all on hard-surfaced track. It is therefore suitable for pushchairs or other wheels and will be firm underfoot, even on the muddiest of days.

You start with a long winding trail through the silent forest, where you may be lucky enough to glimpse the shy deer. When you emerge through the trees on the far side, the Welland Valley opens up before you, and there are excellent views of the Harringworth viaduct away in the west and the distant villages of Rutland to the north. An easy stretch on a quiet road brings you to the old village of Wakerley with its welcoming pub, and it is then but a short stride by road or cross-field path to return to the heart of the wood.

Starting Point: Wakerley Great Wood Car Park, Grid Ref. 961987. The wood lies just west of the A45, 5 miles south of Stamford.

Distance: 4 miles

Terrain: Hard-surfaced track all the way. There is an alternative short cross-field path at the end.

Map: O.S. Landranger 141, Kettering and Corby.

Public Toilets: At Car Park (toilets open in summer only)

Pushchairs: Suitable

Refreshments: The *Exeter Arms* in Wakerley welcomes children and has a large outdoor eating area with children's swings. An ice-cream van may call in the wood on summer weekends. There are picnic tables and barbecues in the wood should you fancy your meal alfresco.

Checklist – Score 2 points for each:

1 A silver birch tree
2 A post with two blue bands
3 A post with two red bands
4 A windmill (look in the distance!)
5 Ferns
6 A haystack
7 Tree shields (plastic tubes preventing animals nibbling young trees)
8 A tractor
9 A railway viaduct
10 A red telephone box
11 A weather-cock
12 These buildings (they are lime kilns which were built by prisoners of war and never used)

and for 5 points – a deer!

Total Score _____

The Walk

⇒ From any of the car parking areas, walk back towards the main entrance to the woods. Where the road swings left to the entrance, turn right and go through a green metal barrier on to the hard-surfaced track beyond. You are now on the horse permit trail and you should keep straight ahead on it, ignoring paths going off on both sides.

Q1   Along this stretch you will pass a willow tree, with a green wooden post in the ground giving you its two names. What are they?

_____

Score 2 points ____

⇒ After nearly a mile, the hard track swings sharply to the left – a grassy track is coming in from the right here. Keep to your hard track. Shortly it takes a sharp bend to the right and soon after you come to another corner to the left. Here you should leave the track and follow the horse trail markers which direct you up a narrow path ahead passing between some concrete boulders. 20 metres beyond the boulders, at a track crossing, leave the horse trail and turn right, slightly doubling back on yourself.

☺ The surface here is still concrete underneath. We are now on the site of an old airfield.

⇒ Follow this track, bearing slightly left to cross a broad concreted area. Bearing again left from this area will bring you on to a wide concrete track, which turns a corner and then leads you out of the wood. Keep to the track with the woodland edge on your right. Soon a waymarked footpath comes in on your left, and you bear to the right, still on concrete. Continue until you are on a wide concreted area where there may be a haystack, and have passed the narrow finger of woodland, Long Wood, on your right. Now turn sharp right on to a track, which leads through the shorter scrubby trees at the end of the wood.

☺ The scrubland soon ends and suddenly you have a wide view of the Welland Valley as you descend the hill. Away to the left you can see the Harringworth viaduct – how long did it take to construct this monster, and how many bricks did they use? The railway line is now used only for freight, but you could possibly see a train crossing it. Ahead of you is the

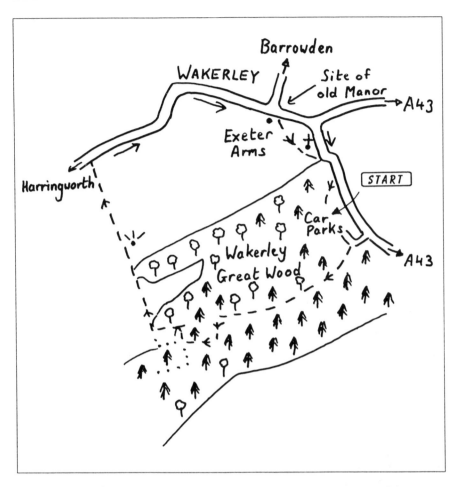

pretty village of Barrowden – if you visit it afterwards, you will find lovely stone houses and a fine pub around a village green with a duck pond. There are plenty of ducks, too! Between you and Barrowden is the River Welland, which here is the border between Northamptonshire and the smallest county in Britain, Rutland. There's a lot to see as you come down this hill!

Q2   As you walk down, several church spires come into view. (No, they can't all be seen from the top!) For 1 point each, how many spires can you see? _____

Score _____

⇒ At the bottom of the track, turn right on the road and follow it into Wakerley. It is a quiet road with very little traffic, and it follows the line of the river and a disused railway line. Keep to the road through the village as far as the Exeter Arms on the right-hand side.

Q3   As you pass through the village of Wakerley, how many *yellow* fire hydrants can you see? They are certainly well-prepared for fire here! Score one point for each yellow hydrant.

Score _____

☺ The field opposite the *Exeter Arms* has some very interesting looking humps and hollows in it. You are looking at the remains of a fine manor house once owned by the Cecil family, who took the title 'Earl of Exeter' -now you know where the pub got its name! The manor house was abandoned by them after a series of misfortunes some 300 years ago, and has since fallen to ruin. The Cecil family still live at Burghley House near Stamford.

Q4   From the *Exeter Arms*, look down the road to Barrowden on the left. On the right of the road stands a very curious house with a white-painted top half. What do you think this house was originally?

_____

Score 3 points _____

⇒ If you are returning by road, walk on past the Exeter Arms to the road junction. Here turn right and continue uphill past the church. If you can manage a cross-field path, go up the steps from the corner of the pub car park and follow the Jurassic Way signs across the fields past the back of the church.

☺ Whatever route you take, the church door is worth a look—you won't get inside, as the church is now redundant and locked. The elaborate iron-work on the door is seen on other churches in the Rockingham Forest area and it is said that the door was made for protection. In the Middle Ages, bandits roamed the forest and at times the villagers needed a safe refuge! Bandits wouldn't break that door down so easily!

⇛ On reaching the road, turn right and follow it round the corner and past the little car park, (you could go into the forest here, but it's easy to get lost!) until you come to a 'Jurassic Way' signpost directing you back into the forest on your right. The post is well-concealed, but you will find it at the junction of deciduous and coniferous woodland. The short path now leads you back to a broader track and the main car parks.

A frosty morning in the woods

Well done! And here comes the score . . .

More than 28   Impressive!

20 – 28   A fine score!

Under 20   Hmmm!

Walk 20: Yarwell

Where stepping stones bridge the river

In the far north of the county, the twin villages of Nassington and Yarwell are full of charm and interest. The walk starts from Yarwell Mill on the River Nene. There is a small caravan park here where day visitors are welcomed for a small fee. You can park on the picnic area beside the lake where there is plenty of space for playing and a few children's swings. From here, on a fine day, you can wander up to the old mill and watch boats passing through the lock, perhaps savouring an ice cream from the van which regularly calls in summer.

The route climbs up from the mill and crosses fields to reach the attractive village of Yarwell with its lovely old stone houses. More than a century ago, when the nearby limestone quarries were most productive, the village was a centre for stonemasons, and their work is still in evidence!

Leaving Yarwell on the 'main' road, we quickly branch off along a wooded lane to reach Nassington. The village is steeped in history. There are Roman remains and a Saxon cemetery was uncovered just to the south. King Canute had a royal manor in Nassington in Saxon times and was a frequent visitor. As you walk through the village, you will pass the oldest inhabited house in Northamptonshire, the Prebendal Manor. It was built around 1230, and would have been the home of a 'Prebendary' of Lincoln Cathedral who administered the surrounding area as part of the cathedral's estate. There are many other interesting old houses in Nassington, and among them, two inns all welcoming children and a well-stocked village shop.

From Nassington the return is on the Nene Way beside the river to Yarwell Mill. The original route of the Nene Way crosses the river on stepping stones at one point – fun for the adventurous, but there is an alternative, should you feel this is not for you!

Starting Point: Yarwell Mill, Grid Ref. 074974. From the A605, turn left 3 miles north of Oundle, following the signs to Fotheringhay. Continue through Fotheringhay to Nassington, and, at the end of the village, under the railway bridge, take the right-hand fork to the mill.

Parking: In the picnic area at Yarwell Mill (small charge) or, alternatively, above the mill, on Mill Road in the village of Yarwell.

Distance: 3½ miles

Map: O.S. Landranger 142, Peterborough

Terrain: Cross-field paths, a rough lane, and pavements in villages.

Public Toilets: At Yarwell Mill

Pushchairs: Fine at Yarwell Mill and on village pavements, otherwise not suitable.

Refreshments: There are three pubs en route – *The Angel* at Yarwell and *The Black Horse* and *The Queen's Head*, both at Nassington. All welcome children inside, and each has a small outside garden area.

Checklist – Score 2 points for each

1   A Life Belt

2   A Mill Stone

3   A Weather Vane

4   A Yellow Footprint

5   A house from *The Wind in the Willows*

6   A picture of a swan on a river

7   The date 1998 in a brick circle

8   A sundial

9   A rabbit

10   A magpie

11   A wooden bench

12   A horse

Total Score _____

The Walk

⇒ From the picnic area, walk up to the mill and follow the road, keeping the lock on your left-hand side. Take the first footpath on the right as you climb the hill. This takes you across fields to reach the road at Yarwell. Turn right and follow the road through the village.

☺ On your way through the village you pass the church, and every church has an interesting story! In the chancel of this church is the tomb of one Sir Humphrey Bellamy who died in 1715. He was a poor boy who had decided to go to London to try to make his fortune. On the way he fell ill, and the good people of Yarwell took him in and nursed him back to health. Eventually he continued on his journey to London, and in due time he was made an Alderman and became rich. (Yes, this certainly sounds like the story of Dick Whittington!) He never forgot Yarwell, and in his will left money to be distributed annually to the poor of the parish.

Boats at Yarwell Mill

Q1   In addition to the parish church there is another church in Yarwell. What sort of church is it? _____

Score 3 points _____

⇛ Continue along the main street to its junction with the Nassington road, and here turn left on the footpath beside the road. Ignore the first footpath on the right, and continue almost to the top of the hill, where a byway forks off on the right. This byway is a wooded lane which leads you into Nassington. When you reach the village, keep straight ahead and follow the road all the way through.

Q2   How many thatched houses do you pass on your way through the village? Score 1 point for each house.

Score _____

☺   On you right you will pass the Prebendal Manor House, dated 1230, and well worth a visit if it is open. Opposite is the Church of St Mary. There is lots of interest here, too. If you go inside, look for the carved stone

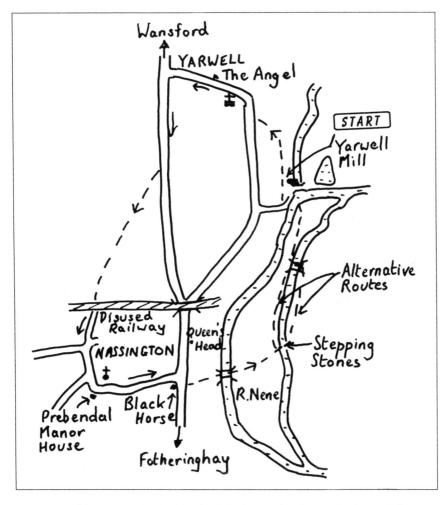

preaching cross in the North aisle (opposite the main door). It is over 1000 years old!

⇒ Continuing along the main street, you eventually come to a road junction, with the *Black Horse* public house on the right.

Q3 The *Black Horse* is a very old pub. What date was it built? _____

Score 2 points_____

⇒ The centre of the village with the shop and the *Queen's Head* public house lies to the left, but you should turn right at this junction, and then take the first footpath on the left (Nene Way). Follow the signs across the river and then across two more fields. In the next field you have a choice! On your right, the old route of the Nene Way takes you on stepping stones across the river. The path then follows the river bank and returns over a bridge some distance farther along. If you feel the stepping stones are too adventurous, you can continue along the path ahead, keeping the river on your right, to reach the same bridge.

Q4 These stepping stones are man-made. What shape are their tops?

_____

Score 2 points ____

⇒ From the bridge, another field path and a short track, all on the Nene Way, return you to Yarwell Mill.

_____

Well done! Now add up your score . . .

More than 23   Excellent observation!

16 – 23   A very good try!

Under 16   You may have had your eyes closed! Try again!

Answers to Questions

Walk 1 – Oundle

Ql 25th April 1990 (on plaque on the first post on the left)

Q2 There are 10 stiles in all

Q3 A butterfly

Q4 There are lots of Horse Chestnuts (conker trees) in Ashton.

Q5 There is a depth measurer – like a big white ruler – standing in the river.

Q6 There are at least four of these door knockers – and probably more.

Q7 The post is in the bushes to the left of the path

Walk 2 – Brigstock

Ql 2 church spires can be seen

Q2 Bramble / dog rose / hawthorn / blackthorn / and others

Q3 To protect the young trees from nibbling by deer.

Q4 A cow

Q5 A sundial

Walk 3 – Great Addington

Ql There are 10 spires in all, but that of Rushden is very distant and not always visible.

Q2 No. 66 is Blacksmith Cottage

Q3 Salmon (it tells you on the notice board)

Q4 Swans, coots, mallards and grebes are common. There may well be others.

Walk 4 – Castle Ashby

Ql The church was completed in 1534 – there should be a notice in the porch.

Q2 It is called *Threefold*

Q3 The cows are Friesians

Q4 1865

Q5 This text is on the garden terrace wall, to the right of the house.

Q6 There are seven horseshoes.

Walk 5 – Stoke Bruerne

Ql 20 miles (on canalside milepost just before tunnel)

Q2 It is a ventilation shaft for the canal tunnel.

Q3 Well, I counted five – but more could have been added!

Q4 Cycling (on notice by gate)

WALK 6 – Pattishall

Q1 Well, people can always take down or put up bird tables – so I don't know the exact number. But there are at very least three . . .

Q2 It was once an inn called *The Boot.*

Q3 You tied your horse to the ring while you climbed the steps to mount it!

Q4 A sundial

Q5 The Silver Jubilee of Queen Elizabeth II

Q6 A train

Walk 7 – Silverstone

Ql There are at very least four – but you may well have seen more.

Q2 There are 23 telegraph poles! Being clever, you will have noticed that you started at no. 4, and then the numbers followed up to 13, giving 10 poles. The next pole was again 13, and the numbers then ran down to 1 – another 13 poles, making 23 in total.

Q3 1744

Q4 Forest Enterprise

Walk 8 – Aynho

Q1 There are four flights of steps

Q2 A yellow (golden?) weathercock

Q3 The clock is on the wall of the first house on the right – The Old

School House. The baby pelicans are roosting on the top of the large house on the right at the far end of the village.

Q4 There are four gateways – three on the track and one on the main road.

Q5 The tree is just behind the wall towards the road end of the track, not far from the grey house.

Q6 The animal (a wolf?) has an arrow through its neck.

Walk 9 – Middleton Cheney

Q1 Well, I thought there were 17 shell signs, but then I could be wrong, too! A few either side of that will be fine!

Q2 There are at least three spires – those of Middleton Cheney, Banbury and, away to the south, the elegant but distant spire of King's Sutton – but there may be more!

Q3 These are ash trees – the commonest trees in Northamptonshire. But they don't usually look quite like this!

Q4 They are yew trees, often found in churchyards.

Q5 There is 'The Old School House', just before the school.

Walk 10 – Boddington

Q1 I saw four lifebelts – but there could be more or fewer when you go.

Q2 It is an Ash tree.

Q3 There are at least three – The Old Bakehouse, The Old Forge and The Old Post Office.

Q4 There are 3 windows.

Walk 11 – Fawsley

Q1 The trees are oaks.

Q2 1686 is on the house beside the church; 1722 is on the house beside the little green; 1966 is on the house next to the village stores.

Q3 A house and a fir tree

Q4 Well, I hope you saw lots – but they can be difficult to spot in the trees.

Q5 There are four wooden gates.

Q6 The ha-ha was made to keep the animals out of the church.

Walk 12 – Flore

Q1 I hope you did see some 'Roses and Castles' – although unfortunately we couldn't arrange for a suitable boat to be waiting for you! Look out for these traditional paintings whenever you are by a canal.

Q2 Originally, narrow boats were pulled by horses, who walked on the towpath. The towropes rubbing on the corners of the bridge have made the grooves you see.

Q3 London

Q4 They are lime trees.

Q5 There are 13 stiles in all!

Q6 The Nene Valley Project

Walk 13 – Brixworth

Q1 The bridge has seven arches (although, to be honest, I couldn't count seven from the track).

Q2 There were six seats when I last went this way – although more could have been added since.

Q3 The symbols are a bike, a wheelchair, a footprint and a horseshoe.

Q4 A golden weathercock.

Q5 The village stocks, which were once used to punish wrongdoers.

Walk 14 – West Haddon

Q1 There is an old pump on the road from the playing field, before you reach the junction. The remains of a pump are in the bus shelter at Winwick, while the third, brightly-painted, pump stands beside the road a little farther up the hill before Winwick Hall.

Q2 The fire insurance plaque is on The Old Post House.

Q3 Six pipes cross the stream.

Q4 Those who gave their lives in the 1914-1918 War.

Q5 Queen Victoria

Q6 Winwick Hall was built in 1850, and the Baptist Chapel in 1882. So the Hall was built first by 32 years.

Walk 15 – Barby

Ql I counted 14 stiles – but I think I missed one or two! So if you got anything like that score, you can have 5 points!

Q2 There was once a pub here called *The Devon Ox.*

Q3 There are several wattle and daub walls – you may have seen them beside the path up to the church or on Middle Street to the right of the shop.

Q4 It is a holly tree.

Q5 There is a row of carved faces just below the top. Can you see anyone you recognise?

Walk 16 – Welford

Q1 I think I saw five different kinds. How did you get on?

Q2 There is a depth measurer near the far end of the causeway.

Q3 Well, I lost count – but I think there were at very least six!

Q4 It is a horse-chestnut tree.

Q5 The church is dedicated to St Helen.

Q6 A radio mast

Walk17 – Arthingworth

Ql There were five seats when I was last here – but I suppose that could have changed since!

Q2 It is a triangular meadow – as it says on the sign.

Q3 Dragonflies. There is a notice about it on the gate below the bridge.

Q4 418 metres – on a sign at the entrance.

Q5 They are Hall Farm and Church Farm (both on the right as you go down the hill) and then Glebe Cottage Farm, opposite the pub.

Walk 18 – East Carlton

Q1 The bungalow is called *Ninesprings.*

Q2 I think I could see five – but you may have found others! Walking towards Middleton, behind you is Ashley, ahead are Great Easton and Caldecott, while much farther back is Lyddington. Just peeping over the hill directly opposite across the valley is Medbourne.

Q3 1862 is on the old houses opposite the kissing gate where you reached the road; 1992 is on some garages on the right; 1868 is the date on the restored Forge.

Q4 The trees are horse chestnuts.

Q5 The initials are I.H.P. – the initials of one of the Palmer family.

Q6 I hope there was a male mallard posing for you to identify!

Walk 19 – Wakerley

Q1 The tree is a Sallow or Goat Willow.

Q2 You can see four spires – those of Wakerley, Barrowden, Seaton (on the hill to the left) and, as you near the bottom of the hill, Harringworth, close to its viaduct.

Q3 There are five yellow hydrants.

Q4 There is actually more than one house here and they once were the station buildings which stand beside the now disused railway track.

Walk 20 – Yarwell

Q1 A Methodist Church

Q2 There are two thatched houses.

Q3 1674

Q4 Square

DERBYSHIRE
WALKS with CHILDREN

William D. Parke

NORTHUMBRIA
WALKS with CHILDREN

Stephen Rickerby

"Walks with Children" books are available for the following areas:

Cheshire

Derbyshire

Gloucestershire

Greater Manchester

Lake District (North)

Lake District (South)

Northumbria

Snowdonia

Yorkshire Dales

These are the ideal companions for family walks in the countryside. Each book is £6.95 except those for Cheshire and Greater Manchester, which are £7.95.